普通高等教育经管类专业系列教材

会 计 英 语

（第2版）

张 淼 王文杰 主编

清华大学出版社
北 京

内 容 简 介

本书是一本为会计英语教学而编写的专业基础教材,按会计学专业主干课程的架构共设11章,主要内容包括:会计概述;交易事项;应收账款;存货与销货成本;投资;有形资产、自然资源和无形资产;负债;所有者权益;收入与费用;财务报表;审计。各章由基本知识、核心词汇、拓展阅读和练习题组成。其中,核心词汇可以帮助学生自主学习,减少全英文教材阅读给学生带来的理解上的困难;拓展阅读部分介绍了会计的基本理论、重点和难点,对中外会计准则进行对比,并通过融入会计学中的人生哲理,潜移默化地实现对学生的人生教化和价值引领;练习题可以帮助学生练习并巩固相关知识点。

本书可作为高等院校本科和高职高专会计、审计、财务管理等专业的会计英语课程教材,也可作为广大财会从业人员学习会计英语的专业图书。

本书提供配套电子课件、教案和习题答案。

本书封面贴有清华大学出版社防伪标签,无标签者不得销售。
版权所有,侵权必究。举报:010-62782989,beiqinquan@tup.tsinghua.edu.cn。

图书在版编目(CIP)数据

会计英语 / 张淼,王文杰主编. —2版. —北京:清华大学出版社,2023.8(2025.1重印)
普通高等教育经管类专业系列教材
ISBN 978-7-302-64477-4

Ⅰ.①会… Ⅱ.①张…②王… Ⅲ.①会计-英语-高等学校-教材 Ⅳ.①F23

中国国家版本馆 CIP 数据核字(2023)第 154670 号

责任编辑:高 屾
封面设计:周晓亮
版式设计:方加青
责任校对:马遥遥
责任印制:刘 菲

出版发行:清华大学出版社
网   址:https://www.tup.com.cn,https://www.wqxuetang.com
地   址:北京清华大学学研大厦A座   邮   编:100084
社 总 机:010-83470000   邮   购:010-62786544
投稿与读者服务:010-62776969,c-service@tup.tsinghua.edu.cn
质 量 反 馈:010-62772015,zhiliang@tup.tsinghua.edu.cn

印 装 者:北京嘉实印刷有限公司
经   销:全国新华书店
开   本:185mm×260mm   印   张:11.5   字   数:245千字
版   次:2019年6月第1版 2023年9月第2版   印   次:2025年1月第4次印刷
定   价:45.00元

产品编号:102032-01

前　言

随着国际经济贸易的发展和资本的国际流通，经济全球化已经日益深化。而会计学科作为企业经济管理的重要工具，尤其需要与国际接轨。社会主义市场经济的到来使得我国在对外贸易、国际融资、跨境投资等领域飞速发展，培养新型的会计国际化人才已经成为财经类高校的一项重要任务。

本书以国际会计准则和美国会计准则为导向，既有基础会计的基本理论和中级财务会计的进阶会计知识，也有审计学科的基本知识，让学生通过学习会计实务中英文的习惯表达和丰富的会计英语词汇，提高阅读英语会计文献和使用英语处理常规会计业务的能力，培养运用英语进行会计业务操作的能力，满足学生毕业后的工作岗位的实际需要。

本书按会计学专业主干课程的架构共设11章，主要内容包括：会计概述；交易事项；应收账款；存货与销货成本；投资；有形资产、自然资源和无形资产；负债；所有者权益；收入与费用；财务报表；审计。第2版更新了陈旧的数据，与时俱进地更换了大量案例，并在拓展阅读模块中融入会计学的人生哲理，以"立德树人"为根本，帮助教师在开展专业教育的同时培养和塑造学生的价值观，潜移默化地实现对学生的人生教化和价值引领。

本书的创新之处在于每章设置核心词汇、拓展阅读和练习题模块。核心词汇以中英文对照的方式呈现，使学生能够自主学习，减少全英文教材阅读给学生带来的理解上的困难。拓展阅读部分内容丰富，英语较为薄弱的学生可以通过这一部分把握每章内容的精髓，非会计专业的学生可以通过这一部分了解会计的基本理论、重点和难点，还可借助其中对中外会计准则的对比，明确相关会计问题在不同准则下的处理差异。练习题编排合理，题型多样，帮助学生练习并巩固相关知识点。本书提供配套教学资源，包括电子课件、教案和习题答案，可通过扫描右侧二维码获取。

教学资源

本书由张淼、王文杰任主编，负责全书的编写工作。其中，第1~8章由张淼编写，第9~11章由王文杰编写。此外，参与编写的人员有李佳钰、陈潇瑜、卢禹燕、彭月、王慧凝、徐旖聪、杨媛等。为了进一步提升本书的质量，东北财经大学会计学院的傅荣教授作为本书的主审，将其多年来对国内外企业会计准则的研究成果融入本书的内容体系。

在本书的编写过程中，编者们得到了所在学校领导、老师和相关部门的大力支持与帮助，在此表示衷心的感谢！由于时间仓促，水平有限，本书难免存在不足，恳请专家和读者批评指正。

编　者
2023年8月

目 录

Chapter 1　Fundamentals of Accounting ·· 1
　　Spotlight ·· 2
　　Text ·· 3
　　　　1.1　Who Use Accounting Data ·· 3
　　　　1.2　Forms of Enterprise Organizations ·· 3
　　　　1.3　Two Kinds of Accounting ·· 5
　　　　1.4　Accounting Standards ·· 6
　　　　1.5　Accounting Assumptions and Principles ·································· 7
　　　　1.6　Elements of the Financial Statements ···································· 9
　　　　1.7　Accounting Equation ·· 11
　　　　1.8　Accrual Basis and Cash Basis ·· 11
　　Core Words ·· 12
　　Extended Reading ·· 13
　　Exercises ·· 15

Chapter 2　Transaction ·· 19
　　Spotlight ·· 20
　　Text ·· 20
　　　　2.1　Definition of Transaction ·· 20
　　　　2.2　Accounting Elements ·· 21
　　　　2.3　Journal Entry ·· 23
　　　　2.4　Accrual Accounting ·· 24
　　　　2.5　Posting ·· 27
　　　　2.6　Trial Balance ·· 29
　　　　2.7　Close the Books ·· 29
　　Core Words ·· 32
　　Extended Reading ·· 33
　　Exercises ·· 34

Chapter 3 Receivables 39

  Spotlight 40
  Text 40
    3.1 Variety of Receivables 40
    3.2 Account for Uncollectible Account 41
    3.3 Measurement of Uncollectible Account 42
    3.4 Notes Receivable 44
    3.5 Accounts Receivable Turnover 46
  Core Words 46
  Extended Reading 47
  Exercises 48

Chapter 4 Inventory and Cost of Goods Sold 53

  Spotlight 54
  Text 54
    4.1 Classifications of Inventory 54
    4.2 Cost of Goods Sold 54
    4.3 Gross Profit 55
    4.4 Accounting for Inventory 55
    4.5 Various Inventory Costing Methods 56
    4.6 Summary of Inventory 59
    4.7 Effects of Inventory Errors 59
    4.8 Lower-of-Cost-or-Market Rule 60
    4.9 Inventory Turnover 61
  Core Words 62
  Extended Reading 62
  Exercises 64

Chapter 5 Investment 67

  Spotlight 68
  Text 68
    5.1 Debt Investments 68
    5.2 Share Investments 69
    5.3 Short-term Investments and Long-term Investments 72
  Core Words 74
  Extended Reading 74
  Exercises 76

Chapter 6　Plant Assets, Natural Resources, and Intangible Assets　79

- Spotlight　80
- Text　81
  - 6.1　Plant Assets　81
  - 6.2　Capitalized Expenditures and Immediate Expenses　82
  - 6.3　Account for Depreciation of Plant Assets　82
  - 6.4　Revaluation of Plant Assets　85
  - 6.5　Disposal of Plant Assets　87
  - 6.6　Natural Resources and Depletion　88
  - 6.7　Intangible Assets　89
- Core Words　93
- Extended Reading　94
- Exercises　96

Chapter 7　Liabilities　99

- Spotlight　100
- Text　101
  - 7.1　Accounting for Current Liabilities　101
  - 7.2　Liabilities with Uncertainty　106
  - 7.3　Accounting for Long-term Liabilities　107
- Core Words　111
- Extended Reading　112
- Exercises　114

Chapter 8　Stockholders' Equity　119

- Spotlight　120
- Text　121
  - 8.1　Background and Definition of Owners' Equity　121
  - 8.2　The Classification of Stocks　123
  - 8.3　Issuing Stock　124
  - 8.4　Cash Dividends　125
  - 8.5　Stock Dividends　126
- Core Words　128
- Extended Reading　129
- Exercises　131

Chapter 9　Revenues and Expenses　135
Spotlight　136
Text　137
- 9.1　Accrual Basis and Cash Basis　137
- 9.2　Measurement of Sales Revenue　138
- 9.3　Merchandise Returns and Allowances　138
- 9.4　Cash and Trade Discounts　139
- 9.5　Expenses　140
Core Words　142
Extended Reading　143
Exercises　145

Chapter 10　Financial Statements　149
Spotlight　150
Text　150
- 10.1　Overview of Financial Statements　150
- 10.2　Formats for Financial Statements　152
Core Words　156
Extended Reading　156
Exercises　158

Chapter 11　Auditing　161
Spotlight　162
Text　163
- 11.1　Audit Framework　163
- 11.2　Professional Ethics and Codes of Conduct　165
- 11.3　Standards of Reporting　167
Core Words　169
Extended Reading　170
Exercises　172

Chapter 1
Fundamentals of Accounting

Spotlight

Accounting is commonly referred to as the language of the business world. In business, accounting always serves as a communication tool for numerical information. It is a method that businesses utilize as a means to convey financial information to both their employees and the public. Previously, the accounting languages varied across countries. Today, only two major accounting languages are in use—one in the United States, and the other in Europe and many other parts of the world.

Accounting is the important basic work of modern enterprises. It focuses on providing useful information to help enterprises make decisions through a series of accounting procedures. **Identifying, recording, and communicating** the financial transactions of an organization to interested parties are the three fundamental activities of accounting. The quality of fundamental accounting directly impacts the assessment of internal and external conditions of an enterprise. By analyzing financial information, enterprise managers can forecast and evaluate the business situation, and control economic activities. Additionally, they can evaluate the different plans of the enterprise to ensure that it can capitalize on opportunities and mitigate potential risks.

In this book, you will find that the fundamental principles of accounting are consistent. Therefore, by studying these principles presented in this text, you will be well-prepared to comprehend the financial outcomes of companies around the world. This chapter begins with the fundamentals of accounting, which encompasses various information users, forms of enterprise organization, accounting types, accounting standards, the basic assumptions of accounting, the accounting elements, and the accounting equation. It should be emphasized that accounting is essential for all types of corporate organizations.

Text

1.1 Who Use Accounting Data

The financial information that users need depends on the type of decisions they are required to make. Financial information users can generally be classified into two main categories: internal users and external users.

1.1.1 Internal Users

Internal users of accounting information are individuals or groups within a company or an organization who use financial information to **plan, organize, and run** a business. It is related to the daily operations and management of the business.

Some examples of internal users include managers, executives, employees, and the board of directors.

1.1.2 External Users

External users are individuals or organizations who are not part of a company but have a need or desire to access its financial information. They may use this information for various purposes, such as making investment decisions, assessing the company's creditworthiness, or conducting research. External users rely on the accuracy and completeness of a company's financial information to make informed decisions about their interactions with the company.

Examples of external users include investors, creditors, suppliers, customers, regulatory bodies, and the general public.

1.2 Forms of Enterprise Organizations

While many accounting processes apply to all types of companies, variations in the legal structure of a company result in differences in accounting for owners' equity. In this context, we will examine three fundamental forms of ownership structure for business entities: proprietorship, partnership, and corporation.

1.2.1 Proprietorship

A **proprietorship** can also be called a **sole trader**. Most often, it is a business owned by one person and the owner usually serves as the manager as well. In consequence, proprietorships tend to be retail establishments such as local stores, restaurants, and individual professional businesses such as dentists or attorneys who operate alone.

Starting a proprietorship typically requires only a relatively small amount of capital. The proprietor, who owns the business, is accountable for all profits and losses, and assumes full **personally liable** for all debts of the business.

1.2.2 Partnership

A **partnership** has two or more persons as co-owners. It is a cooperative relationship between people or groups who agree to share responsibility for achieving some specific goal. Usually, a partnership also bears **unlimited joint and several liabilities**. The most basic form of partnership could be when a group of individuals come together to create a business.

A professional entity that provides paid service to its clients with specialized knowledge and skills may form a specialized general partnership, which can be called limited liability partnership. In limited liability partnership, each partner is liable only for his own actions and those under his control. The number of partners can be huge. International accounting firm PwC for example, has over 400 partners in China and Singapore region.

1.2.3 Corporation

A **corporation** is a type of business that is established as a distinct legal entity under corporate law, with ownership divided into transferable shares. The owners of a corporation undertake the limited liability for debts with registered capital, meaning that creditors of the corporation (such as banks or suppliers) can make claims only against the corporate assets, and not the personal assets of the owners. Conversely, in proprietorships and partnerships, owners are typically held personally liable for any obligations of the business.

In most large corporations, ownership shares are publicly traded as stocks. This implies that the company offers ownership shares to the public for purchase, with buyers becoming shareholders or stockholders. Shareholders may transfer all or part of its shares to other investors on the stock exchange. Such corporations usually have a multitude of shareholders numbering in the thousands.

A **limited liability company** (LLC) is a legal form of a company that bears limited liability to its owners in many jurisdictions. However, the LLC's ownership structure differs from the corporation, as its members do not hold shares but rather have legal interests proportional to their investment. When members of an LLC sell their ownership, they are selling their own interests rather than stock. China does not allow unlimited liability companies to exist.

The differences of organization forms are shown in EXHIBIT 1-1.

EXHIBIT 1-1 The Differences of Organization Forms

Item	Proprietorship	Partnership	Corporation	LLC
Owner	One owner	Two or more owners	Shareholders	Members
Personal liability of owner for business debts	Personally liable	Personally liable	Not personally liable	Not personally liable

1.3 Two Kinds of Accounting

1.3.1 Management Accounting

Management accounting, also known as **managerial accounting**, is the process of analyzing and interpreting financial information and data to provide internal users with the tools they need to make informed business decisions. The main focus of managerial accounting is to provide relevant and timely financial information to managers within an organization to help them make better decisions related to planning, controlling, and decision-making. It is tailored to meet the specific needs of internal management. It can help managers in developing and monitoring budgets, assessing the profitability of products and services, evaluating investment decisions, and identifying cost-saving opportunities.

The scope of managerial accounting includes a range of activities such as budgeting, cost analysis, variance analysis, performance measurement, and forecasting. It provides managers with detailed information about the financial performance of specific departments or projects within the organization, as well as insight into trends and potential future scenarios.

1.3.2 Financial Accounting

Financial accounting is a branch of accounting that focuses on the preparation and reporting of a company's financial statements to external users, such as investors, creditors, and regulatory agencies. The primary objective of financial accounting is to provide reliable, relevant, and accurate financial information about a company's performance, financial position, and cash flows.

Financial accounting involves the **recording, classifying, summarizing,** and **interpreting** of financial transactions and events to generate financial statements, including the balance sheet, income statement, and cash flow statement. These statements provide a comprehensive overview of a company's financial performance, including its revenues, expenses, assets, liabilities, and equity.

Financial accounting is guided by various accounting principles, standards, and guidelines, such as the Generally Accepted Accounting Principles (GAAP) in the United States and the International Financial Reporting Standards (IFRS) in many other countries. The use of these standards helps to ensure consistency, transparency, and comparability of financial information across different companies and jurisdictions.

1.4 Accounting Standards

1.4.1 International Accounting Standards Board

The **International Accounting Standards Board** (IASB) is an independent, global accounting standard-setting organization which headquartered in London, UK, with its 15 board members drawn from around the world. The IASB develops and promotes the use of high-quality financial reporting standards, known as International Financial Reporting Standards (IFRS), which are used by companies and organizations around the world.

The IASB is responsible for developing and maintaining the IFRS, which cover a range of financial reporting topics, including revenue recognition, leasing, financial instruments, and accounting for intangible assets. These standards are used by companies and organizations in over 140 countries, including many of the world's largest economies.

The IASB works closely with national accounting standard-setting bodies and other stakeholders, including investors, regulators, and accounting professionals, to ensure that its standards meet the needs of users of financial statements and are relevant, reliable, and globally accepted.

1.4.2 Financial Accounting Standards Board

The **Financial Accounting Standards Board** (FASB) is an independent, non-profit organization based in Norwalk, Connecticut, USA. The FASB's mission is to establish and improve financial accounting and reporting standards to provide useful information to investors and other users of financial reports. The FASB is recognized as the authoritative standard-setting body for financial accounting and reporting in the United States. The FASB develops and maintains the Generally Accepted Accounting Principles (GAAP), which are widely used by public and private companies, not-for-profit organizations, and government entities in the United States.

The FASB's standards cover a range of financial accounting and reporting topics, including revenue recognition, leases, and financial instruments. The FASB also provides guidance on emerging issues and conducts research to inform its standards-setting process. Its standards are used by thousands of companies, investors, and other stakeholders to make informed financial decisions.

1.5 Accounting Assumptions and Principles

1.5.1 The Entity Assumption

The entity assumption requires that the transactions of each entity are accounted for separately from the transactions of all other organizations and persons. It is the most basic accounting concept. The accounting entity concept is applied to all organization forms of businesses: proprietorship, partnership, and corporation.

1.5.2 The Going-concern Assumption

The going-concern assumption is the assumption that ordinarily an entity persists indefinitely. In another word, an entity will remain in operation long enough to use existing assets for their intended purpose. Under this assumption, an entity reports its long-term assets, such as plant and equipment, based on their historical cost rather than the liquidation value.

1.5.3 The Time-period Concept

For accounting information to be useful, it must be made available at regular intervals. **The time-period concept** ensures that accounting information is reported at regular intervals. The basic accounting period is one year, for example, an entity prepares annual financial reports. An entity also prepares financial statements for an interim period, such as a month, a quarter, and a semiannual period.

1.5.4 The Monetary Unit Assumption

The monetary unit assumption assumes that all financial transactions and events are recorded in a common monetary unit, such as a dollar or euro. In China, we record transactions in RMB while Americans record transactions in US dollars. The value of RMB changes all the time. A rise in the general price level is called *inflation*. A decline in the general price level is called *deflation*. Under the monetary unit assumption, we ignore inflation and deflation. Accountants assume that the currency value is stable.

1.5.5 Fundamental Qualitative Characteristics

The **fundamental qualitative characteristics** are a set of characteristics that describe the key attributes of financial information that make it useful for decision-making.

Relevance: Relevant financial information is capable of making a difference in the decisions made by users. To be relevant, information must be timely, have predictive value, and have confirmatory value.

Faithful representation: Financial information should represent faithfully the economic phenomena it purports to represent. To achieve faithful representation, information must be complete (it includes all necessary information), neutral (free from bias), and accurate (it really happened).

The fundamental qualitative characteristics play a crucial role in ensuring financial information is valuable for decision-making. Financial reporting that includes information that is relevant and accurately represents the underlying economic phenomena can assist investors, creditors, and other stakeholders in evaluating an entity's financial position and performance, allowing them to make well-informed decisions regarding their interactions with the entity.

1.5.6 Measurement Principles

Measurement principles are a set of guidelines used to measure and report financial transactions in financial statements. Generally, it includes historical cost principle and fair value principle.

- **The Historical Cost Principle**

This principle requires that assets and liabilities be recorded at their historical cost (amount paid or received at the time of acquisition). Historical cost reflects the original cost of an asset or liability and is considered a reliable and objective measurement method. However, it does not reflect the current value of an asset or liability.

For example, an example of the historical cost principle would be a company purchasing a piece of land for $100,000 in 2022. According to the historical cost principle, the company would record the land on its financial statements at the original purchase price of $100,000. Even if the land has significantly appreciated in value and is worth millions of dollars in the current market, the company would continue to report the land at its original cost of $100,000 on its financial statements.

- **The Fair Value Principle**

The fair value principle is an accounting principle that requires assets and liabilities to be reported at their estimated current market value. In other words, the fair value principle requires companies to report their assets and liabilities on their financial statements at the price that they could be sold for on the open market. The fair value principle is intended to provide more accurate and relevant information to investors and other users of financial statements by reflecting the current economic value of a company's assets and liabilities.

For example, if a company owns a stock that has increased in value since it was purchased, the fair value principle would require the company to report the stock on its financial statements at its current market value, which may be higher than its original cost. Similarly, if a company has a liability that has increased in value since it was incurred, the fair value principle would require the company to report the liability on its financial statements at its current market value, which may be higher than the original amount owed.

1.6 Elements of the Financial Statements

1.6.1 Financial Position

- **Asset**

As mentioned earlier, assets refer to the resources owned by a business. The business uses its assets to carry out various activities, such as production and sales. According to FASB, "An asset is a probable future economic benefit obtained or controlled by an entity as a result of a past transaction or event." That means an **asset** is an economic resource controlled by the entity as a result of past events, which is expected to produce a future benefit, such as cash, land, plant, and inventory. A coffee shop can identify the coffee machine as an asset, since coffee produced by coffee machine can be sold for money.

- **Liability**

Liabilities are claims against assets—that is, existing debts and obligations. According to FASB, "A liability is a probable future sacrifice of economic benefits arising from present obligations of an entity to transfer assets or provide services as a result of a past event or transaction." That means a **liability** is a present obligation of the entity arising from past events, which will result in an outflow of resource from the entity. They are debts that are payable to creditors. For example, a bank loan can be identified as a liability, since an entity needs to pay off the principal and interest within a certain period of time.

- **Owners' Equity**

Equity means ownership. In accounting, equity is the residual value or interest of the most junior class of investors in assets, after all liabilities are paid. If liabilities exceed assets, a negative equity exists. It is a residual value, which equals to assets minus liabilities. There are two main sub-parts in owners' equity: **paid in capital and retained earnings.**

1.6.2 Business Performance

- **Revenue**

An entity creates **revenue** by provide goods and services to customers. In many countries, revenue is referred to as turnover. In accounting, revenue is often referred to as the "top line" due to its position on the income statement at the very top. This is to be contrasted with the "bottom line", which denotes net income. Revenues will increase the net income as well as the owners' equity of an entity.

- **Expense**

In common usage, an **expense** is an outflow of money to another person or group to pay for an item or service, or for a category of costs. For a tenant, rent is an expense. For students, tuition fee is an expense. Buying food, clothing, and furniture is often referred to as an expense.

In accounting, expense has a very specific meaning. It is an outflow of cash or other valuable assets from a person or company to another person or company. According to International Accounting Standards Board, an expense is defined as "decreases in economic benefits during the accounting period in the form of outflows or depletion of assets or incurrences of liabilities that result in decreases in equity, other than those relating to distributions to equity participants". **Expenses** are decreases in economic benefits during the accounting period in the form of outflow of assets. Expenses will decrease the net income as well as the owners' equity of an entity.

- **Income**

Income is also called **profit** or **earnings**. Income refers to the money that an individual or a household receives in exchange for providing goods or services or from investments. It can take various forms, such as wages or salaries earned from employment, profits earned by a business, interest or dividends earned on investments, rental income from property, or other sources.

In economics, income is often classified into different categories such as gross income, net income, disposable income, and discretionary income. Gross income is the total income earned before any deductions, while net income is the income remaining after deducting taxes and other expenses. Disposable income is the income available after deducting taxes and other necessary expenses such as housing, food, and transportation. Discretionary income is the income left over after deducting necessary expenses, which can be used for non-essential expenses such as entertainment or vacations.

1.7 Accounting Equation

The **accounting equation**, also known as the balance sheet equation, is a fundamental principle in accounting that describes the relationship between a company's assets, liabilities, and equity. The accounting equation can be expressed as follows:

Assets = Liabilities + Equity

In other words, the assets of a company are equal to the sum of its liabilities and equity. This equation must always be in balance, which means that the total value of the assets must be equal to the total value of the liabilities and equity. In addition, the other accounting equations are shown in EXHIBIT 1-2.

EXHIBIT 1-2　The Other Accounting Equations

Assets=Liabilities + Owners' equity
Assets=Liabilities + Paid in capital + Retained earnings
Income=Revenues - Expenses

1.8 Accrual Basis and Cash Basis

Accrual basis and cash basis are two methods of accounting used to record and report financial transactions.

1.8.1 Accrual Basis

Accrual basis of accounting is a method in which revenues and expenses are recorded when they are earned or incurred, regardless of when the cash is received or paid.

Under the accrual basis, revenue is recognized when it is earned, and expenses are recognized when they are incurred, even if payment is not received or made until a later date. This method provides a more accurate picture of a company's financial performance, as it reflects the timing of transactions rather than just the cash flow.

1.8.2 Cash Basis

Cash basis is an accounting method that recognizes the impact of transactions on the financial statements only when a company receives or pays cash.

Cash basis of accounting is a method in which revenues and expenses are recorded only when cash is received or paid. Under the cash basis, revenue is recognized when cash is received, and expenses are recognized when cash is paid. This method is simpler and easier to use, but it may not accurately reflect the timing of transactions, especially for companies with significant accounts receivable or accounts payable.

The choice of accounting method can have a significant impact on a company's financial statements and tax liabilities. GAAP requires most businesses to use the accrual basis of accounting. It's important to understand the advantages and disadvantages of each method and choose the one that is best for your business.

Core Words

Internal users	内部使用者
External users	外部使用者
Proprietorship	个人独资企业
Partnership	合伙制企业
Corporation	股份有限公司/集团公司
Limited liability company	有限责任公司
Public company	上市公司
Management/Managerial accounting	管理会计
Financial accounting	财务会计
International Accounting Standards Board (IASB)	国际会计准则委员会
Financial Accounting Standards Board (FASB)	财务会计准则委员会
The entity assumption	会计主体假设
The going-concern assumption	持续经营假设

The time-period concept	会计分期假设
The monetary unit assumption	货币计量假设
The historical cost principle	历史成本原则
The fair value principle	公允价值原则
Asset	资产
Liability	负债
Owners' equity	所有者权益
Revenue	收入
Expense	费用
Income	利润
The accounting equation	会计等式
Accrual basis	权责发生制
Cash basis	收付实现制

Extended Reading

1. 资产

资产是指由企业过去的交易或者事项形成的、由企业拥有或者控制的、预期会给企业带来经济利益的资源。

2. 负债

负债是指由企业过去的交易或事项所形成的、预期会导致经济利益流出企业的现时义务。

3. 所有者权益

所有者权益是指资产扣除负债后由所有者应享的剩余权益,即一个会计主体在一定时期所拥有或可控制的具有未来经济利益资源的净额。会计方程式"资产－负债＝所有者权益"清楚地说明了所有者权益实质上是一种剩余权益,是企业全部资产减去全部负债后的差额,体现企业的产权关系。所有者权益有以下特征:

(1) 所有者权益是企业可长久使用的资金来源，除非发生减资、清算的情况，否则企业不需要偿还所有者权益；

(2) 企业在清算时，所有者权益的清偿列在负债之后；

(3) 所有者权益的满足由企业实现的收益程度决定，所有者凭借所有者权益参与利润的分配。

所有者权益的形成渠道有三条：

(1) 所有者投入的资本；

(2) 所有者投资后的经营增值，如留存收益；

(3) 直接计入所有者权益的利得和损失。

4. 收入

收入是指企业在日常活动中形成的、会导致所有者权益增加的、与所有者投入资本无关的经济利益总流入。

按照中国的会计准则，收入按照业务比重进行确认，主要包括主营业务收入、其他业务收入和投资收益等。而本书基于国际会计准则，收入多按照企业业务类型进行分类，分为服务收入(service revenue)、销售收入(sales revenue)、租金收入(rent revenue)等。具体业务处理会在后续章节讲解。

5. 费用

费用是指企业在日常活动中发生的、会导致所有者权益减少的、与向所有者分配利润无关的经济利益的总流出。在我国会计准则中，习惯将成本和费用分开核算。和收入一样，成本若按照业务所占比重进行分类，可分为主营业务成本和其他业务成本；而国际会计准则习惯不区分，直接使用已销商品成本(cost of goods sold)来进行核算。对于期间费用，我国习惯按照费用的用途将其分为销售费用、管理费用和财务费用，但国际会计准则没有这种分类，而是采用更为细化的会计科目，如广告费(advertising expense)、人工费(salary expense)、房租费(rent expense)等。

6. 利润

会计利润是指企业的总收益减去所有显性成本或者会计成本以后的余额。会计利润是根据会计准则计算的结果。计算的基本方法是，按照实现原则确定一定期间内的收入，按照配比原则确定同一期间的费用成本，将收入与相关费用成本相减，即企业在这一会计期间的利润。为了便于使用者对企业经营情况和盈利能力进行比较和分析，利润表中按多步式对当期的收入、费用和支出项目按性质加以归类，按利润形成的主要环节列示一些中间性利润指标，如营业利润、利润总额、净利润等。

7. 会计起源

关于我国会计的起源，有多种不同的说法。有人讲在夏禹时代，大禹王曾在江南茅山召开过一次诸侯会议，考评诸侯的功绩。这次记功大会刚结束，大禹王便死了。当时，诸侯们举行了隆重的葬礼，把他的遗体安葬在了茅山上。为了纪念大禹和他主持的这次会议，诸侯商定，把茅山更名为"会稽山"，而这个"会稽"就是今天"会计"的起源。

在远古时代，当文字尚未发明的时候，各路出猎者向部落首领报告猎物数目时是用口头语言表达的。不同种类的猎物是多少，总共多少，都要求正确、真实地表达出来，不允许隐瞒和虚报。这种正确而无隐藏的口头计算与报告便构成了"计"字的另一层含义。"零星算之为计，总和算之为会"，是西周时代对会计概念的总结。你认为会计是从什么时候开始出现的呢？

8. 古代会计小故事——傅山与"龙门账"

傅山是明末清初山西帮商人，他参考当时官厅会计的"四柱清册"记账方法，设计出一种适用于民间商业的会计核算方法——"龙门账"。龙门账的要点是将全部账目划分为进、缴、存、该四大类。"进"指全部收入；"缴"指全部支出；"存"指资产并包括债权；"该"指负债并包括业主投资。当时的民间商业一般只在年终办理结算(称之为年结)，年结就是通过"进"与"缴"的差额，同时通过"存"与"该"的差额，平行计算盈亏。"进"大于"缴"就是盈利，反之则为亏损。它与"存""该"的差额相等。也就是说，进-缴=存-该。傅山将这种双轨计算盈亏并检查账目平衡关系的会计方法形象地称为"合龙门"，"龙门账"因此而得名。"龙门账"的诞生标志着我国复式簿记的开始。

Exercises

1. Which enterprise organization has only one owner? (   )

    A. Sole trader.　　　　　　　　　B. Partnership.
    C. Limited liability company.　　　　D. Corporation.

2. The final result of which kind of accounting is the financial statement? (   )

  A. Management accounting.　　　　　B. Financial accounting.

  C. Auditing.　　　　　　　　　　　　D. Cashier.

3. Why does a going-concern assumption exist? (   )

  A. Because the business will not go bankrupt.

  B. Because we can't predict the risk of a corporate.

  C. Because the accounting methods of bankruptcy liquidation are different.

  D. Because it is the most basic accounting principle.

4. Which costing method is the most reliable? (   )

  A. Historical cost.　　　　　　　　　　B. Fair value.

  C. Replacement cost.　　　　　　　　　D. Present value.

5. Which one is not the interim period of financial statement? (   )

  A. Annual report.　　　　　　　　　　B. Semiannual report.

  C. Quarter report.　　　　　　　　　　D. Month report.

6. Which of the following is the nature of asset? (   )

  A. Asset is controlled by an entity.

  B. Asset can bring the entity future benefit.

  C. An asset is a probable future economic benefit obtained or controlled by an entity as a result of a past transaction or event.

  D. Asset is something owned by an entity due to a present event.

7. If the entity has $8,000 in asset, and $2,000 in liability, how much is the owners' equity? (   )

  A. $6,000.　　　　　　　　　　　　　B. $10,000.

  C. $3,000.　　　　　　　　　　　　　D. $2,000.

8. If the entity has $10,000 in expense, and $4,000 in revenue, what is the business performance? (   )

  A. $14,000 net income.　　　　　　　　B. $14,000 net loss.

  C. $6,000 net income.　　　　　　　　　D. $6,000 net loss.

9. Which accounting subject is affected by net income? (   )

  A. Inventory.　　　　　　　　　　　　B. Cash.

  C. PPE.　　　　　　　　　　　　　　　D. Retained earnings.

10. When will an entity use cash basis? (   )

  A. An entity never uses cash basis.　　　　B. When identifies revenue.

C. When identifies expense.   D. When making statement of cash flow.

11. Which of the following is the nature of liability? (   )

   A. Liability is an obligation of the entity.

   B. Liability can bring the entity future loss.

   C. Liability is a present obligation of the entity arising from past events, which will result in an outflow of resource from the entity.

   D. Liabilities are debts that are payable to debtors.

12. Which of the following is not the internal users? (   )

   A. Managers.   B. Executives.

   C. Employees.   D. Suppliers.

13. Which characteristics are Fundamental qualitative? (   )

   A. Faithful representation.   B. Similarity.

   C. Relevance.   D. Interactive.

14. What are the differences among proprietorship, partnership, limited liability company, and corporation?

15. What are the differences between financial accounting and management accounting?

16. Identify the missing amount for each equation.

Total assets	=	Total liabilities	+	Stockholders' equity
?		180000		200000
300000		100000		?
250000		?		140000

17. Classify the following items as an Asset(A), a Liability(L), or a Stockholders' equity(E).

_____	Account receivable	_____	Account payable
_____	Merchandise inventory	_____	Notes payable
_____	Supplies	_____	Equipment
_____	Common stock	_____	Salary payable
_____	Retained earnings	_____	Dividend
_____	Prepaid expenses	_____	Land

18. Indicate whether each of the six statements presented below is true or false. If false, indicate how to correct the statement.

1. The three steps in the accounting process are identification, recording, and communication. (   )

2. The two most common types of external users are investors and company officers. (   )

3. Managerial accounting activities focus on reports for internal users. (   )

4. The primary accounting standard-setting body headquartered in London is the International Accounting Standards Board (IASB).(   )

5. The historical cost principle dictates that companies record assets at their cost. In later periods, however, the fair value of the asset must be used if fair value is higher than its cost. (   )

6. Relevance means that financial information matches what really happened; the information really existed. (   )

Chapter 2
Transaction

Spotlight

Accounting practice, commonly known as bookkeeping, involves the systematic recording and processing of financial transactions. This process typically starts with completing original documents and culminates in the preparation of financial statements. With the evolution of market economy and increasing complexity of financial transactions, the ability to accurately and reasonably handle each business transaction has become a necessary skill for many accountants. Therefore, bookkeeping has gained significance beyond its procedural aspects, and now focuses on how to improve the process for better outcomes.

Caroline and her friends open a healthcare center named "Good for Your Health". In the daily business, a series of economic operations will happen, such as accepting investment, purchasing fixed asset, purchasing materials, providing service, and paying expense. How can we record these items professionally? What are the requirements in the accounting standards when recording these transactions?

Text

In the previous chapter, we provided an overview of the fundamental components of accounting, including the types of users, accounting assumptions and accounting equations. In this chapter, we will provide a more detailed explanation of these elements of accounting and explain the process of recording transactions using journal entries.

2.1 Definition of Transaction

A financial **transaction** is an agreement or communication, carried out between a buyer and a seller to exchange an asset for payment. It involves a change in the status of the finances of two or more businesses or individuals. The buyer and seller are separate entities or objects, often involving the exchange of items of value, such as information, goods, services, and money. It is still a transaction if the goods are exchanged at one time, and the money at another. This is known as a two-part transaction: part one is giving the money; part two is receiving the goods. A **transaction** is any event that has a financial impact on business and can be measured reliably.

There are two elements in the definition of transaction:

(1) As accounting equation is an identical equation, each transaction affects at least two accounting elements.

(2) Financial impact determines what kind of accounting elements to use.

2.2 Accounting Elements

2.2.1 Assets

An **asset** is a resource controlled by the entity as a result of the past and from which future economic benefits are expected to flow to the entity.

Cash is a term used to refer to money, particularly money that is readily available. It generally refers to current assets that can be accessed immediately and includes physical currency, such as banknotes and coins, as well as deposits and checks. In bookkeeping and finance, cash is considered to be a current asset.

Accounts receivable are current asset accounts showing amounts payable to an entity by customers who have made purchases of goods or services on credit.

Notes receivable are similar to accounts receivable, but a note receivable is more binding because the customer signed the note. Notes receivable represent claims for which formal instruments of credit are issued as evidence of debt, such as a promissory note. The credit instrument normally requires the debtor to pay interest and extends for a period of 30 days or longer. Notes receivable are considered as current assets if they are to be paid within 1 year, and non-current if they are expected to be paid after 1 year. In China, the due time of the note is usually within 6 months.

Inventory is also called merchandise inventory. It is the merchandise that a shop holds on hand which includes raw materials, semi-finished goods, and finished goods.

Land account shows the cost of the land that an entity uses in its operations, especially when the land is used for farming or building.

Building account shows the cost of purchased office buildings, or manufacturing plants of an entity.

Equipment account shows the cost of tools and machines that an entity needs to use in daily production and operation activities, such as manufacturing equipment and office equipment.

2.2.2 Liabilities

A **liability** is a present obligation of the entity arising from a past event, the settlement of which is expected to result in an outflow from the entity of resources embodying economic benefits.

Account payable is a current liability account showing the debt from a credit purchase of inventory or service. If it is an account receivable to a seller, it is an account payable to a buyer.

Note payable is a note promising to pay a certain amount of money at a certain time, carrying interest. If it is a note receivable to a seller, it is a note payable to a buyer. It is also used when money is borrowed from the bank.

2.2.3 Stockholders' Equity

Stockholders' equity is also called **owners' equity**. It is the residual interest in the assets of an entity after deducting all its liabilities.

Common stock is a type of investment that gives shareholders ownership in a corporation and the right to vote on certain company decisions. Shareholders may also receive dividends if the company is profitable, but owning common stock comes with certain risks due to potential fluctuations in stock value.

Retained earnings account shows the cumulative net income earned by an entity, minus its cumulative net losses and dividend over the entity's lifetime. Retained earnings are the portion of a company's profits that have been kept by the company instead of being paid out as dividends to shareholders. They are often reinvested in the business to fund future growth or to pay off debt.

Dividend is the money declared and paid to the owners by an entity. It is optional, which means the board of directors can decide to pay dividend or not. Dividend is not an expense. It will never affect net income.

2.2.4 Revenue

Revenues are increases in economic benefits during the accounting period in the form of inflows of assets or decreases of liabilities that result in increases in equity, other than those relating to stockholders' investment. The entity uses as many revenue accounts as needed, such as **sales revenue**, **service revenue**, **rent revenue**, and **interest revenue**.

2.2.5 Expense

Expenses are decreases in economic benefits during the accounting period in the form of outflows or depletion of assets or increases of liabilities that result in decreases in equity, other than those relating to distributions to equity participants. An entity needs a separate account for each type of expense, such as **cost of goods sold**, **salary expense**, **rent expense**, **utilities expense**, and **advertising expense**.

2.3 Journal Entry

Caroline and a few friends opened a healthcare center near a community, named "Good for Your Health". During March, 2022, the following transactions happened.

Transaction 1

Caroline and her friends invested $800,000 to the healthcare center, and issued common stock to the stockholders.

  Dr: Cash   800,000
    Cr: Common stock   800,000

Transaction 2

The healthcare center purchased land for a new location and paid cash of $200,000.

  Dr: Land   200,000
    Cr: Cash   200,000

Transaction 3

The healthcare center bought some medical supplies in cash, $6,000.

  Dr: Supplies   6,000
    Cr: Cash   6,000

Transaction 4

The healthcare center earned $3,500 by providing medical service for customers and received cash.

  Dr: Cash   3,500
    Cr: Service revenue   3,500

Transaction 5

During this month, the healthcare center paid cash for the following expenses: equipment rent, $1,500; employee salary, $2,500; utilities, $800; advertisement fee, $900.

  Dr: Rent expense   1,500

Salary expense	2,500
Utilities expense	800
Advertising expense	900
Cr: Cash	5,700

Transaction 6

Caroline paid $8,000 for a vacation to Italy.

It is a personal transaction, and it is not recorded.

Transaction 7

The healthcare center sold some land which bought in Transaction 2 at its cost.

Dr: Cash	200,000
Cr: Land	200,000

Transaction 8

The healthcare center declared a dividend, and paid cash of $12,000

Dr: Dividend	12,000
Cr: Cash	12,000

2.4　Accrual Accounting

During day-to-day operations, transactions do not always involve the immediate receipt or payment of cash by an entity. In order to accurately reflect these types of transactions, adjustments are necessary to align them with the appropriate accounting period, as required by the accrual basis of accounting.

The purposes of **adjusting**:

♦ Measure income.

♦ Update the balance sheet.

2.4.1　Adjusting

Explicit transactions are observable events such as cash receipts and disbursement, credit purchases, and credit sales that trigger nearly all day-to-day routine entries.

Implicit transactions are events that do not generate source documents or visible evidence of the events. We do not recognize such events in the accounting records until the end of an accounting period.

Adjustments are end-of-period entries which assign the financial effects of implicit transactions to the appropriate period of time.

2.4.2 Types of Adjusting

- **Deferral**

1) Expiration of unexpired cost and prepaid expense

Transaction 9

On March 2, 2022, the healthcare center purchased $8,000 of supplies, and at the end of the month, there were $6,500 of supplies left.

March 2
  Dr: Supplies   8,000
    Cr: Cash   8,000

March 31
  Dr: Supplies expense   1,500
    Cr: Supplies   1,500

Transaction 10

The healthcare center paid $9,000 for 3 months' rent on March 1.

March 1
  Dr: Prepaid rent expense   9,000
    Cr: Cash   9,000

March 31
  Dr: Rent expense   3,000
    Cr: Prepaid rent expense   3,000

April 30
  Dr: Rent expense   3,000
    Cr: Prepaid rent expense   3,000

May 31
  Dr: Rent expense   3,000
    Cr: Prepaid rent expense   3,000

2) Unearned revenue

Transaction 11

The healthcare center received $12,000 for 3 months' rent on March 1.

March 1
  Dr: Cash   12,000
    Cr: Unearned rent revenue   12,000

March 31
  Dr: Unearned rent revenue 4,000
    Cr: Rent revenue 4,000
April 30
  Dr: Unearned rent revenue 4,000
    Cr: Rent revenue 4,000
May 31
  Dr: Unearned rent revenue 4,000
    Cr: Rent revenue 4,000

- **Accrual**

1) Accrual of unrecorded expenses

Transaction 12

The healthcare center borrowed money from the bank, and the interest for March was $850.

Accrual interest
  Dr: Interest expense 850
    Cr: Interest payable 850
Pay interest
  Dr: Interest payable 850
    Cr: Cash 850

Another example is salary payable.

2) Accrual of unrecorded revenue

Transaction 13

The healthcare center lent money to another entity, and the interest for March was $900.

Accrual interest
  Dr: Interest receivable 900
    Cr: Interest revenue 900
Receive interest
  Dr: Cash 900
    Cr: Interest receivable 900

- **Depreciation**

Transaction 14

On March 1, 2022, the healthcare center purchased a piece of equipment at $9,000. The useful life of the equipment is 5 years, and its residual value is 0. Suppose the healthcare center uses the straight-line method.

March 31

    Dr: Depreciation expense   150

        Cr: Accumulated depreciation   150

2.5 Posting

Accountants make use of a journal, which is a sequential record of transactions, but the journal does not provide information about the amount of cash or accounts receivable held by the entity. However, a T-account can give such information.

For example:

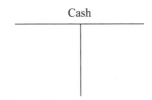

The left side means **debit,** and the right side means **credit**.

A ledger is a grouping of all the T-accounts.

The process from journal to ledger is called **posting.**

The ledger of the healthcare center in March, 2022 is shown in EXHIBIT 2-1.

EXHIBIT 2-1   The Ledger of the Healthcare Center in March, 2022

```
                Assets              =        Liabilities           +    Stockholders' equity

                 Cash                       Unearned rent revenue            Common stock
     (1)  800,000  | (2) 200,000          (11) 4,000 | (11) 12,000                   | (1) 800,000
                   | (3)   6,000                     | Bal  8,000                    | Bal 800,000
     (4)    3,500  | (5)   5,700
     (7)  200,000  | (8)  12,000             Interest receivable                Dividend
                   | (9)   8,000          (12)  850  | (12)  850        (8) 12,000   |
                   | (10)  9,000                     | Bal     0        Bal 12,000   |
     (11) 12,000   | (12)    850
     (13)    900   |                                                         Service revenue
     Bal  774,850  |                                                                 | (4) 3,500
                                                                                     | Bal 3,500

                 Land
     (2)  200,000  | (7) 200,000                                              Rent revenue
     Bal       0   |                                                                 | (11) 4,000
                                                                                     | Bal  4,000
```

(Continued)

| Assets | = | Liabilities | + | Stockholders' equity |

Supplies
(3)	6,000		
(9)	8,000	(9)	1,500
Bal	12,500		

Prepaid rent expense
| (10) | 9,000 | (10) | 3,000 |
| Bal | 6,000 | | |

Interest receivable
| (13) | 900 | (13) | 900 |
| Bal | 0 | | |

Accumulated depreciation
| | | (14) | 150 |
| | | Bal | 150 |

Interest revenue
| | | (13) | 900 |
| | | Bal | 900 |

Rent expense
(5)	1,500		
(10)	3,000		
Bal	4,500		

Salary expense
| (5) | 2,500 | | |
| Bal | 2,500 | | |

Utilities expense
| (5) | 800 | | |
| Bal | 800 | | |

Interest expense
| (12) | 850 | | |
| Bal | 850 | | |

Advertising expense
| (5) | 900 | | |
| Bal | 900 | | |

Supplies expense
| (9) | 1,500 | | |
| Bal | 1,500 | | |

Depreciation expense
| (14) | 150 | | |
| Bal | 150 | | |

2.6 Trial Balance

After posting journal entries to the ledger, the next step is the preparation of a trial balance. A **trial balance** is a list of all accounts with their balances. It summarizes all the account balances for the financial statements and shows whether total debits equal total credits, as shown in EXHIBIT 2-2.

EXHIBIT 2-2   Trial Balance of the Healthcare Center on March 31, 2022

Account Title	Balance Debit	Balance Credit
Cash	774,850	
Land	0	
Supplies	12,500	
Prepaid rent expense	6,000	
Interest receivable	0	
Accumulated depreciation		150
Unearned rent revenue		8000
Interest payable		0
Common stock		800,000
Dividend	12,000	
Service revenue		3,500
Rent revenue		4,000
Interest revenue		900
Rent expense	4,500	
Salary expense	2,500	
Advertising expense	900	
Utilities expense	800	
Supplies expense	1,500	
Interest expense	850	
Depreciation expense	150	
Total	816,550	816,550

2.7 Close the Books

2.7.1 Temporary Account

Accounts like revenues and expenses which relate to a limited period are called **temporary accounts**, such as revenues, expenses, and dividends.

2.7.2 Permanent Account

Accounts like assets, liabilities, and equities which carry over to the next period are called **permanent accounts**. Permanent accounts are not closed at the end of the accounting period.

Close the books means preparing the ledger accounts to record the next period's transactions by making closing entries that summarize all balances in the revenue and expense accounts and transferring the balances to retained earnings.

(1) Debit each revenue account for the amount of its credit balance, and credit retained earnings for the sum of revenues.

Dr: Service revenue	3,500
Rent revenue	4,000
Interest revenue	900
Cr: Retained earnings	8,400

(2) Credit each expense account for the amount of its debit balance, and debit retained earnings for the sum of the expenses.

Dr: Retained earnings	11,200
Cr: Rent expense	4,500
Salary expense	2,500
Advertising expense	900
Utilities expense	800
Supplies expense	1,500
Interest expense	850
Depreciation expense	150

(3) Credit the dividends account for the amount of its debit balance, and debit retained earnings.

Dr: Retained earnings	12,000
Cr: Dividends	12,000

The process of posting temporary accounts is shown in **EXHIBIT 2-3**.

Transaction

EXHIBIT 2-3 Posting Temporary Accounts to Retained Earnings

Rent expense	
1,500	
Adj. 3,000	
Bal. 4,500	Clo. 4,500

Salary expense	
Adj. 2,500	
Bal. 2,500	Clo. 2,500

Advertisin gexpense	
Adj. 900	
Bal. 900	Clo. 900

Utilities expense	
Adj. 800	
Bal. 800	Clo. 800

Supplies expense	
Adj. 1,500	
Bal. 1,500	Clo. 1,500

Interest expense	
Adj. 850	
Bal. 850	Clo. 850

Depreciation expense	
Adj. 150	
Bal. 150	Clo. 150

Service revenue	
	Adj. 3,500
Clo. 3,500	Bal. 3,500

Rent revenue	
	Adj. 4,000
Clo. 4,000	Bal. 4,000

Interest revenue	
	Adj. 900
Clo. 900	Bal. 900

Retained earnings	
Clo. 11,200	17,000
Clo. 12,000	Clo. 8,400
	Bal. 2,200

Dividend	
Adj. 12, 000	
Bal. 12, 000	Clo. 12,000

Why do we need to close the temporary accounts?

Because the balance of a temporary account only relates to one account period.

Core Words

Transaction	交易事项
Cash	现金
Accounts receivable	应收账款
Notes receivable	应收票据
Inventory	存货
Land	土地
Building	建筑物
Equipment	设备
Account payable	应付账款
Note payable	应付票据
Common stock	股本
Retained earnings	留存收益
Dividend	分红
Sales revenue	销售收入
Service revenue	服务收入
Rent revenue	租金收入
Interest revenue	利息收入
Cost of goods sold	已销商品成本
Salary expense	工资费用
Rent expense	租金费用
Utilities expense	公共事业费用
Advertising expense	广告费
Journal entry	会计分录
Adjusting	调账
Explicit transaction	显式业务
Implicit transaction	隐式业务
Unexpired cost	未消耗成本
Prepaid expense	待摊费用
Unearned revenue	预售收入
Unrecorded expense	未入账费用
Unrecorded revenue	未入账收入
Depreciation	折旧

Posting	过账
Ledger	账簿
Trial balance	试算平衡
Temporary account	临时账户
Permanent account	长期账户
Close the books	结账

Extended Reading

1. 会计科目表

国际会计准则没有具体的会计科目表，因此，在美国，对于会计处理应采用什么分录，没有明确要求，通常情况下根据业务的明细进行记账。而在我国，则必须使用会计科目表中的科目填制记账凭证。

2. 试算平衡

试算平衡是指在借贷记账法下，利用借贷发生额和期末余额(期初余额)的平衡原理，检查账户记录是否正确的一种方法。本章仅演示了发生额试算平衡，即"全部账户借方发生额合计=全部账户贷方发生额合计"。试算平衡的理论基础就是会计基本恒等式，即"资产=负债+所有者权益"。如果试算不平衡，说明记账工作发生了差错；如果试算平衡，则说明记账工作基本正确。但是试算平衡方法并不能发现记账过程中的全部错误，比如漏记、重记、记账方向颠倒、用错会计科目等。

3. 生活中的"等式"

会计中重要的等式是"资产=负债+所有者权益"，强调等式左右的平衡。左侧是拥有的资源，右侧是承担的责任和义务。从资产负债表角度来看，同学们要有"先天下之忧而忧，后天下之乐而乐"的抱负，和"苟利国家生死以，岂因祸福避趋之"的报国情怀。只有讲求奉献，才能得到越来越多的净权益。希望通过会计恒等式与报表，激发同学们的家国情怀。作为当代大学生，应当志存高远，奋发图强。在今后的工作中，应做到爱岗敬业，诚实守信，坚持原则，操守为重，不做假账，秉持社会主义核心价值观，做合格会计人。

4. 领会党的二十大精神，苦练"金刚钻"

站在新的历史起点，我们要深刻领会党的二十大精神内涵，认真贯彻落实党中央关于进一步加强财会监督的重大决策部署，把学习成果转化为行动实践。新时代财会监督人员担负的职责比以往任何时候都要重大，这对财会监督人员提出了更高的要求：一是要求我们必须切实提高政治站位，从政治和全局的高度推动中央重大决策部署的贯彻落实，高质量完成财政部安排的财会监督各项工作；二是要求我们提升专业能力，苦练"金刚钻"，不仅要掌握财政、财务、会计方面的监督知识，还需要具备较强的学习能力和综合素质；三是要求我们坚持发扬斗争精神，练就过硬斗争本领，不断提高系统思维能力，既敢于斗争又善于斗争，既斗争又合作，做到在原则问题上寸步不让，在策略问题上灵活机动。

真正的精英并不是天才，而是付出了更多努力的人。当你停步不前时，别忘了别人还在奔跑。所以，敬告那些取得一些成绩就安于现状的人们，不要再优哉游哉地荒废时间了。作为新时代财务人员，我们应把握好每一个学习机会，苦练专业知识，提升个人素养，强化财务、会计等方面的知识，好好打造属于自己的"金刚钻"。

Exercises

1. Which account type usually has a debit balance? (   )

   A. Asset. B. Liability.

   C. Owners' equity. D. Revenue.

2. Which account type usually has a credit balance? (   )

   A. Asset. B. Liability.

   C. Revenue. D. Both B and C.

3. Which is the most liquid one in current asset? (   )

   A. Cash. B. Account receivable.

   C. Inventory. D. Short-term investment.

4. Which of the following is a non-current liability? (   )

   A. Account payable. B. Salary payable.

   C. Income tax payable. D. Long-term debt.

5. Accounts receivable had a beginning balance of $3,000. During the period, there were debit postings of $1,000, and credit postings of $500. What is the ending balance? (　)
   A. $3,500 debit.　　　　　　　　　　B. $3,500 credit.
   C. $1,500 debit.　　　　　　　　　　D. $1,500 credit.

6. Accounts payable had a beginning balance of $2,000. During the period, there were debit postings of $1,000, and credit postings of $200. What is the ending balance? (　)
   A. $2,800 debit.　　　　　　　　　　B. $2,800 credit.
   C. $1,200 debit.　　　　　　　　　　D. $1,200 credit.

7. Which of the following statements about trial balance is true? (　)
   A. If the trial balance is balanced, the accounts must be correct.
   B. The trial balance can help to find out all errors in bookkeeping.
   C. In trial balance, total debits equal total credits.
   D. Trial balance is useless.

8. The beginning cash balance is $2,500. At the end of the month, the ending balance is $6,000. If cash paid out during the month is $15,000, what is the amount of cash receipt? (　)
   A. $3,000.　　　　　　　　　　　　B. $6,000.
   C. $18,500.　　　　　　　　　　　 D. $9,000.

9. Purchasing an equipment on account will (　).
   A. increase asset　　　　　　　　　B. decrease asset
   C. decrease liability　　　　　　　　D. increase expense

10. Providing service on account will (　).
    A. increase liability　　　　　　　　B. decrease liability
    C. increase asset　　　　　　　　　D. decrease asset

11. Which of the following statements about an account is true? (　)
    A. The right side of an account is the debit or increase side.
    B. An account is an individual accounting record of increases and decreases in specific asset, liability, and equity items.
    C. There are separate accounts for specific assets and liabilities, but only one account for equity items.
    D. The left side of an account is the credit or decrease side.

12. Which of the following is not part of the recording process? (　)
    A. Analyzing transactions.
    B. Preparing an income statement.

C. Entering transactions in a journal.

D. Posting journal entries.

13. A trial balance (   ).

    A. is a list of accounts with their balances at a given time

    B. proves the journalized transactions are correct

    C. will not balance if a correct journal entry is posted twice

    D. proves that all transactions have been recorded

14. AAA Company completed the following transactions during May, 2022.

May	1	Received $50,000 cash, and issued common stock.
	1	Paid $15,000 cash for a land to use as a building site.
	1	Paid office rent, $550 for this month.
	5	Purchased $600 of office supplies on account.
	7	Performed service for customers on account, $400.
	13	Collected $600 from customers on account.
	14	Paid off account payable $650.
	20	Borrowed $9,000 from the bank, and signed a note payable.
	25	Paid the following expenses: salary, $4,000; utilities, $700.
	31	Recognized rent expense for this month.
	31	Paid cash dividend to stockholders, $1,200.

Record the transactions in the journal.

15. Please prepare the related entries according to the following accounting events.

    (1) Jan. 1 X company received $ 40,000 cash, and issued common stock.

    (2) Jan. 1 X company had taken a loan from the bank and signed a note for $180,000.

    (3) Jan. 1 X company paid $20,000 cash for land and intended to use it as a factory building site.

(4) Jan. 2 X company purchased $16,000 of raw materials on credit.

(5) Jan. 6 X company performed $2,800 of service for customers on account.

(6) Jan. 7 a customer returned two machines due to the incorrect color for cash at a total of $650.

(7) Jan. 13 X company collected $2,400 from customers on account.

(8) Jan. 20 X Company paid the following expenses: rent, $2,100; insurance, $1,500; utilities, $1,400.

(9) Jan. 31 X Company paid $68,000 of salary to staff for this month.

Chapter 3

Receivables

Spotlight

Grace Candy Manufacturer is a company specializing in candy production. The factory processes candy to all kinds of fashionable candy toys. The company's customers are all over the country. However, because of the long time of transportation and the shortage of funds for the customers, Grace Candy can't always receive the money at once. This leads to a large number of receivables from the company. The receivables of Grace Candy Manufacturer are shown in EXHIBIT 3-1.

EXHIBIT 3-1 The Receivables of Grace Candy Manufacturer

Customers	Total Receivables
AAA	$11,000
BBB	$9,000
CCC	$40,000
DDD	$12,000
EEE	$7,000
Total	$79,000

Can all the receivables be recovered? How can we deal with the unrecoverable part? Is it possible for an enterprise to estimate the amount which cannot be collected?

Text

3.1 Variety of Receivables

Accounts receivable are current asset accounts showing amounts payable to an entity by customers who have made purchases of goods or services on credit.

Notes receivable are similar to accounts receivable, but a note receivable is more binding because the customer signed the note.

- By selling goods and services→Account receivable

  Dr: Account receivable   ×××
   Cr: Sales revenue   ×××

- **By lending money to others→Note receivable**
  Dr: Note receivable   ×××
      Cr: Cash   ×××

Other receivables include non-trade receivables such as interest receivable, loans to company officers, advances to employees, and income taxes refundable. These do not generally result from the operations of the business. Therefore, they are generally classified and reported as separate items in the statement of financial position.

3.2 Account for Uncollectible Account

By selling on credit, a company runs the risk of not collecting some receivables. It is called **uncollectible-account expense, doubtful-account expense, or bad-debt expense**. How should a company account for these receivables? How do we decide which are collectible and which are not?

There are two basic ways to record an uncollectible account:
- Specific write-off method.
- Allowance method.

3.2.1 Specific Write-off Method

This method of accounting for bad-debt losses assumes all sales are fully collectible until proved otherwise.

Assume that the ending balance of accounts receivable of Grace Candy was $100,000 in 2021 (see EXHIBIT 3-2). In 2022, Grace Candy collected $97,000 back and the rest $3,000 was proved uncollectible.

EXHIBIT 3-2 A Sample of Write-off Method

	Asset	=	Liability	+	Equity
2021	+100,000				+100,000
	Increase in account receivable				Increase in sales
2022 write-off	−3,000				−3,000
	Decrease in account receivable				Increase in bad-debt expense

The journal entry should be:
<u>2022</u>
  Dr: Bad-debt expense   3,000
      Cr: Account receivable   3,000

The specific write-off method is unreasonable for 2 reasons:

(1) Receivables are reported at full amount in 2021, however, the amount of account receivable can not be all collected during the year. Therefore, assets on the balance sheet of 2021 are overstated.

(2) The specific write-off method fails to apply the matching principle of accrual accounting. The bad debt of $3,000 should be the result of 2021, but it is recorded as an expense of 2022.

3.2.2 Allowance Method

The best way to measure bad debts is by the allowance method. This method records collection losses based on estimates developed from the company's collection experience. Grace Candy doesn't need to wait to see whether the customer will pay. Instead, it records the estimated amount as bad-debt expense, and also sets up **allowance for uncollectible accounts, allowance for doubtful accounts, or allowance for bad debts**.

(1) Sales on account:
Dr: Account receivable   100,000
    Cr: Sales revenue   100,000

(2) Provision for bad debt:
Dr: Bad-debt expense   3,000
    Cr: Allowance for bad debt   3,000

(3) Write off:
Dr: Allowance for bad debt   3,000
    Cr: Account receivable   3,000

In this way, expenses are confirmed during the reasonable accounting period.

The next problem is the amount of provision for bad-debt expenses.

3.3 Measurement of Uncollectible Account

The best way to estimate uncollectibles uses the company's history of collections from customers. There are 2 basic ways to estimate uncollectibles:

- Percentage-of-sales method.
- Aging-of-receivables method.

3.3.1 Percentage-of-sales Method

Assume that the total sales revenue of Grace Candy was $40,000 in 2022. Grace Candy estimated that bad-debt expense was 1% of the total revenues.

December 31, 2022

   Dr: Bad-debt expense   400

      Cr: Allowance for bad debt   400

3.3.2 Aging-of-receivables Method

It is an analysis that considers the composition of year-end accounts receivable based on the age of the debt (see EXHIBIT 3-3). The longer an account receivable exists, the higher the risk of bad debt forms.

EXHIBIT 3-3   A Sample of Aging-of-receivables Method

Customers	Total	1 - 30 days	31 - 60 days	61 - 90 days	More than 90 days
AAA	$15,000	$10,000		$5,000	
BBB	$20,000	$15,000	$5,000		
CCC	$40,000	$25,000	$15,000		
DDD	$12,000		$10,000		$2,000
EEE	$7,000			$5,000	$2,000
FFF	$10,000	$10,000			
Total	$104,000	$60,000	$30,000	$10,000	$4,000
Historical bad-debt percentage		1%	2%	10%	30%
Bad-debt allowance	$3,400	$600	$600	$1,000	$1,200

December 31, 2022

   Dr: Bad-debt expense   3,400

      Cr: Allowance for bad debt   3,400

3.3.3 Sale of Receivables to a Factor

A common sale of receivables is a sale to a factor. A **factor** is a finance company or bank that buys receivables from businesses and then collects the payments directly from the customers. Factoring is a multibillion-dollar business.

3.3.4 Credit Sales and Accounts Receivable

Cash sales are important for some companies, but most sales in today's world are on credit. Credit sales create challenges for measuring revenue and managing the company's assets because the company agrees to accept payment in the future for goods or services delivered today. Companies must manage these expected future payments and accounts receivables to ensure their collection in a timely manner.

Credit card use is becoming widespread around the world. ICBC is among the largest credit card issuers in the world. Visa and MasterCard are the credit cards that most individuals use. Three parties are involved when national credit cards are used in retail sales:

(1) the credit card issuer, who is independent of the retailer; (2) the retailer; and (3) the customer. **A retailer's acceptance of a credit card is another form of selling (factoring) the receivable.**

Accounting for Credit Card Sales

The retailer generally considers sales from the use of credit card sales as cash sales. The retailer must pay to the bank that issues the card a fee for processing the transactions. The retailer records the credit card slips in a similar manner as checks deposited from a cash sale.

Recording Charge Card Transactions

In a sense, companies offer cash discounts when they accept charge cards such as **VISA, MasterCard, and American Express**. Why? These credit card companies charge retailers a fee, and the retailers receive an amount less than the listed sales price. Why do retailers accept these cards? There are three major reasons: (1) to attract credit customers who would otherwise shop elsewhere, (2) to get cash immediately instead of waiting for credit customers to pay their accounts, and (3) to avoid the cost of tracking, billing, and collecting customers' accounts.

Deciding When and How to Grant Credit

Competition and industry practice affect whether and how companies offer credit. They offer credit only when the additional earnings on credit sales exceed the costs of offering credit. Suppose 5% of credit sales are bad debts, administrative costs of a credit department are $5,000 per year, and $20,000 of credit sales (with earnings of $8,000 before credit costs) are achieved.

Assume that the company would not receive any of the credit sales without granting credit. Offering credit is worthwhile because the additional earnings of $8,000 exceed the credit costs of [(5% × $20,000) + $5,000] = $6,000.

3.4 Notes Receivable

Notes receivable are more formal than accounts receivable.

Receivables

3.4.1 Key Terms of Notes Receivable

Creditor: The party to whom money is owed. It is usually the bank.

Debtor: A debtor is an entity that owes a debt to another entity. The entity may be an individual, a firm, a government, a company, or another legal person.

Principal: The amount of money borrowed by the debtor.

Interest: It is the cost of borrowing money. On a note, it is usually shown as an annual rate.

Maturity date: The date on which the debtor must pay the note.

Maturity value: The sum of principal and interest on the note.

Term: A fixed period of time from when the note was signed by the debtor to when the debtor must pay the note.

EXHIBIT 3-4 shows a sample note receivable.

EXHIBIT 3-4   A Sample Note Receivable

Note

$6,000

March 1, 2022

Bank of China, Dalian Development Zone

On May 31, 2022
Interest at the annual rate of 8%

Michelle Wang

3.4.2 Account for Notes Receivable

March 1
　Dr: Note receivable　　　　　　　　　6,000
　　Cr: Cash　　　　　　　　　　　　　　　　6,000

March 31
　Dr: Interest receivable　　　　　　　　40
　　Cr: Interest revenue　　　　　　　　　　40

April 30
　Dr: Interest receivable　　　　　　　　40
　　Cr: Interest revenue　　　　　　　　　　40

May 31
　Dr: Cash　　　　　　　　　　　　　　6,120
　　Cr: Note receivable　　　　　　　　　　6,000

Interest receivable	80
Interest revenue	40

3.5 Accounts Receivable Turnover

Investors and company managers compute financial ratios to evaluate the liquidity of a company's accounts receivable. They use the **accounts receivable turnover** to assess the liquidity of the receivables. This ratio measures the number of times, on average, the company collects accounts receivable during the period. It is computed by dividing net credit sales (net sales less cash sales) by the average net accounts receivable during the year. Unless seasonal factors are significant, average net accounts receivable outstanding can be computed from the beginning and ending balances of net accounts receivable.

Core Words

Accounts receivable	应收账款
Notes receivable	应收票据
Bad-debt expense	坏账费用
Specific write-off method	直接销账法
Allowance method	备抵法
Allowance for bad debts	坏账准备
Percentage-of-sales method	销售额百分比法
Aging-of-receivables method	账龄分析法
Creditor	债权人
Debtor	债务人
Principal	本金
Interest	利息
Maturity date	到期日
Maturity value	到期金额
Term	期限
Accounts receivable turnover	应收账款周转率
Credit sales	赊销收入

Extended Reading

1. 应收票据

在中国会计准则中,应收票据是指企业持有的未到期或未兑现的商业票据。也就是说,应收票据通常指"商业汇票",包括"银行承兑汇票"和"商业承兑汇票"两种。而本书中的Note receivable和中文的商业汇票核算范畴不同,在美国等国家/地区,借钱给第三方企业时通常会签订Note receivable。因此,我们习惯在赊销商品和服务时使用Account receivable,对于由借款产生的应收款项,则使用Note receivable。

2. 直接销账法

在我国,对于应收账款,一律需要按照谨慎性原则,采用计提坏账准备的方法,在合理的期间对坏账费用进行确认。如果不计提坏账准备,而采用直接销账法,会导致应收账款产生的会计年度资产被高估,费用被低估,利润被高估。而坏账实际产生的年度资产则被低估,费用被高估,利润被低估。这不符合权责发生制下配比原则的要求。因此我国不允许使用直接销账法。国际会计准则中依然还有这种方法,但应用并不广泛,仅适用于不常有坏账或者坏账数额较小的企业。

3. Net Accounts Receivable

Net accounts receivable is the balance in accounts receivable less the allowance for uncollectible accounts. EXHIBIT 3-5 shows a summary of methods to record bad debts.

EXHIBIT 3-5　Summary of Methods to Record Bad Debts

Method to record bad debts	U.S. GAAP	Tax purpose
Income statement approach: Percentage of sale	Permit	Not permit
Balance sheet approach: percentage-of-account-receivable method	Permit	Not permit
Balance sheet approach: Aging-of-receivables method	Permit	Not permit
Direct write-off method	Not permit	Permit

4. 在学习中保持"世界眼光"

党的二十大报告强调,我们要拓展世界眼光,深刻洞察人类发展进步潮流,积极回应各国人民普遍关切,为解决人类面临的共同问题作出贡献。人类文化和文明发展进步的过程表明,一种文化与异质文化的交流和碰撞、冲突与融合,是保持其生命力、实现自我更新和发展的重要机制，是文化演进与发展的一种带规律性的现象。当今任何民族或国家/地区的文明发展和道德进步，都不可能不受到其他民族或国家/地区的文化或道德文明成果的影响，都不可能脱离人类文明发展的大道。要实现思想政治教育的发展与创新，同样需要把我国的思想政治教育放在世界各国发展进程这个大背景中，用世界眼光去研究和把握当前思想政治教育工作的新形势、新任务、新特点和新规律。

Exercises

1. Which of the following statements is true? (　　)

    A. Accounts receivable are more binding than notes receivable.

    B. Accounts receivable are used when lending money to others.

    C. Specific write-off method is better than allowance method.

    D. Uncollectible account is also called doubtful account.

2. Which of the following statements is false? (　　)

    A. The best way to measure bad debt is allowance method.

    B. Percentage-of-sales method is better than aging-of-receivables method.

    C. It is better to use the combination of percentage-of-sales method and aging-of-receivables method.

    D. The longer an account receivable exists, the higher risk of bad debt forms.

3. Which one is not the basic element of notes receivable? (　　)

    A. Principal. 　　　　　　　　　　B. Maturity date.

    C. Annual rate. 　　　　　　　　　D. Address of debtor.

4. Which of the following is the entry for write-off? (　　)

    A. Dr: Account receivable

    　　Cr: Sales revenue

    B. Dr: Bad-debt expense

    　　Cr: Allowance for bad debt

    C. Dr: Allowance for bad debt

    　　Cr: Account receivable

    D. Dr: Bad-debt expense

    　　Cr: Account receivable

Receivables

5. What is the maturity value of a $40,000, 8%, 6 months note? (   )

   A. $1,600.   B. $3,200.

   C. $41,600.   D. $43,200.

6. The debit balance of accounts receivable is $1,000. The credit balance of allowance for uncollectible accounts is $300. If $100 accounts receivable is written off, what is the balance of receivables after writing off? (   )

   A. $700.   B. $600.

   C. $800.   D. $1,200.

7. The beginning balance of accounts receivable is $15,000. The ending balance of accounts receivable is $18,000. If the total sales of the company during the year is $8,000, how much of the sales is cash sales? (   )

   A. $3,000.   B. $5,000.

   C. $8,000.   D. $10,000.

8. Which of the following statements is true? (   )

   A. For an interim statement, companies use the percentage-of-sales method.

   B. At the end of the accounting period, companies use the percentage-of-sales method.

   C. Both A and B are right.

   D. Both A and B are wrong.

9. Which of the following statements about credit sales is wrong? (   )

   A. It helps to increase in sales.

   B. The risk of credit sales is an uncollectible expense.

   C. A company can avoid bad debts through internal control.

   D. It is important to pursue collections.

10. The beginning balance of allowance for uncollectible accounts is $500. The selling amount during the year is $10,000. If the uncollectible accounts expense is 1% of total sales, what is the ending balance of allowance for uncollectible accounts? (   )

    A. $100.   B. $600.

    C. $400.   D. $500.

11. AAA Company's balance sheet on December 31, 2021, reported:

Accounts receivable	$420,000,000
Allowance for bad debts	($68,000,000)

   AAA Company uses the percentage-of-sales method to estimate bad debts.

Requirement 1

How much does AAA Company expect to collect from its accounts receivable balance as of December 31, 2021?

Requirement 2

Make journal entries for the following transactions in 2022.

(1) If the total sales of AAA Company is $500,000,000 and the estimated percentage is 10%.

(2) Write-offs of uncollectible accounts receivable total $80,000,000. Prepare a T-account for allowance for bad debts with unadjusted balance on December 31, 2022.

(3) On December 31, 2022, it indicates that $45,000,000 is uncollectible at the end of the year. Post to allowance for bad debts, and show its adjusted balance on December 31, 2022.

Requirement 3

Show the balance sheet on December 31, 2022 related to accounts receivable and allowance for bad debts.

Requirement 4

Show the income statement on December 31, 2022 related to bad-debt expense.

12. Accounts receivable at the end of the month are €800,000. Bad debts are expected to be 1.5% of accounts receivable. If allowance for doubtful accounts has a credit balance of €1,000 before adjustment, what is the balance after adjustment? (   )

    A. €7,000.　　　　　　　　　　　B. €11,000.
    C. €12,000.　　　　　　　　　　　D. €13,000.

13. Which of the following statements about Visa credit card sales is incorrect? (   )

    A. The credit card issuer makes the credit investigation of the customer.

B. The retailer is not involved in the collection process.

C. Two parties are involved.

D. The retailer receives cash more quickly than it would from individual customers on account.

14. Receivables are frequently classified as ( ).

    A. accounts receivable, company receivables, and other receivables

    B. accounts receivable, notes receivable, and employee receivables

    C. accounts receivable and general receivables

    D. accounts receivable, notes receivable, and other receivables

15. Accounts and notes receivable are reported in the current assets section of the statement of financial position at ( ).

    A. cash (net) realizable value   B. net book value

    C. lower-of-cost-or-net realizable value   D. invoice cost

16. On December 31, 2022, Carlson Enterprises had accounts receivable of €750,000. On January 1, 2022, allowance for doubtful accounts had a credit balance of €18,000. During 2022, €30,000 of uncollectible accounts receivable were written off. Past experience indicates that 3% of accounts receivable become uncollectible. What should be the bad-debt expense for 2022? ( )

    A. €10,500   B. €30,000

    C. €22,500   D. €34,500

Chapter 4

Inventory and Cost of Goods Sold

Spotlight

Abby opened a bread bakery named Master Chef. There are a large variety of inventories in the bakery. The merchandise inventory is Master Chef's largest asset while the cost of goods sold is the largest expense. How to manage these inventories is the most important issue for the company. However, the cost of the purchase of each batch may be different. The different cost of goods sold may lead to different net incomes. So how can we measure the cost of the inventory sold? How can we measure the ending inventory?

The management of inventory has a significant impact on an entity, especially a commercial enterprise. Reasonable inventory management can help the enterprise to calculate the profit and report the assets correctly. Through the management of the inventory, the enterprise can achieve the ultimate goal of increase of economic benefit.

Text

4.1 Classifications of Inventory

Inventories are also called merchandise inventories. Inventories can include any of the following:

- Finished products.
- Work-in-progress products.
- Materials.
- Purchased goods.

4.2 Cost of Goods Sold

Under the periodic system, calculations for the cost of goods sold start by computing the cost of goods available for sale, the opening inventory for the period plus purchases during the period. From this amount, we subtract the ending inventory value, which is determined by the physical count, to compute the cost of goods sold.

EXHIBIT 4-1 shows the connections and differences between inventory and cost of goods sold.

EXHIBIT 4-1 Inventory and Cost of Goods Sold

Financial statement	Account	Status
Balance sheet	Inventory	On hand
Income statement	Cost of goods sold	Sold

4.3 Gross Profit

For merchandising firms, an initial step in assessing profitability is calculating gross profit. **Gross profit**, also called **gross margin**, is the excess of sales revenue over cost of goods sold. It is the difference between the sales revenue and the cost of goods sold.

Gross profit= Sales revenue−Cost of goods sold

4.4 Accounting for Inventory

There are 2 main types of inventory accounting systems:
- Periodic inventory system.
- Perpetual inventory system.

4.4.1 Periodic Inventory System

In this system, the cost of selling goods is only calculated regularly based on physical inventory, without retaining daily records of sales or inventory units.

The **periodic inventory system** does not involve a day-to-day record of inventories or of the cost of goods sold. Instead, we compute the cost of goods sold and an updated inventory balance only at the end of an accounting period when we take a physical count of the inventory.

Beginning balance+ Newly purchase−Cost of goods sold=Ending balance

Cost of goods sold=Beginning balance+ Newly purchase−Ending balance

Beginning inventory+ Newly purchases−Ending inventory= Cost of goods sold

4.4.2 Perpetual Inventory System

It is a system that keeps a running, continuous record that tracks inventories and the cost of goods sold on a day-to-day basis. The daily record helps managers control inventory levels and prepare interim financial statements. In addition to this continuous record-keeping process, companies periodically physically count and value the inventory. EXHIBIT 4-2 shows a summary of 2 inventory accounting systems.

No matter which method a company chooses to manage its inventory, it should conduct a physical count at least once a year to check on the accuracy of the continuous record.

Journal entry:

(1) Inventory is purchased:

  Dr: Inventory   ×××

    Cr: Cash   ×××

(2) Inventory is sold:

  Dr: Cash   ×××

    Cr: Sales revenue   ×××

  Dr: Cost of goods sold   ×××

    Cr: Inventory   ×××

EXHIBIT 4-2 Summary of 2 Inventory Accounting Systems

Periodic inventory system	Perpetual inventory system
Used for inexpensive goods	Used for all types of goods
Does not keep a running record of all goods bought, sold, and on hand	Keep a running record of all goods bought, sold, and on hand
Inventory counted at least once a year	Inventory counted at least once a year

4.5 Various Inventory Costing Methods

There is a challenge to recognize the cost of goods sold, because the unit price is different every time when purchasing inventory. The inventory record of Master Chef is shown in EXHIBIT 4-3.

EXHIBIT 4-3 The Inventory Record of Master Chef

Inventory			
Beginning balance	20 units@ $20	$400	
Purchase 1	25 units@ $22	$550	Cost of goods sold 55 units@?
Purchase 2	25 units@ $25	$625	
Ending balance	15 units@?		

There are four accepted inventory methods:

- ♦ Specific identification method.
- ♦ Average cost method.
- ♦ First-in, first-out.

Inventory and Cost of Goods Sold

♦ Last-in, first-out.

For each period, accountants must divide the cost of goods available for sale into cost of goods sold and cost of items remaining in ending inventory. Under a perpetual system, we must determine the cost for each item sold. Under a periodic system, we instead must determine the specific costs of the items remaining in ending inventory. In both systems, we must determine the costs of individual items using an inventory valuation method. Four principal inventory valuation methods are commonly used in the United States: specific identification; first-in, first-out (FIFO); last-in, first-out (LIFO); and average cost. Companies reporting under IFRS cannot use LIFO. The most popular method worldwide is the average cost method, and the next most common choice is FIFO. In this section, we will explain and compare these methods.

Compute net incomes and inventory values using the three principal inventory valuation methods allowed by U.S. GAAP and IFRS and the one method allowed only by U.S. GAAP.

4.5.1 Specific Identification Method

Specific identification method concentrates on physically linking the particular items sold with the cost of goods sold that we report. Businesses cost their inventories at the specific cost of the particular unit. This method is relatively easy to use for expensive, low volume merchandise, such as diamond jewelry, vehicles, and houses. This method is too expensive to use for inventory items that have common characteristics.

4.5.2 Average Cost Method

The average cost method is also called the **weighted-average method**. It computes a unit cost by dividing the total acquisition cost of all items available for sale by the number of units available for sale.

$$\text{Weighted average} = \frac{\text{Cost of goods available for sale}}{\text{Units available for sale}}$$

Let's take EXHIBIT 4-3 as an example:

Cost of goods available for sale=20×20+25×22+25×25=1,575($)

Units available for sale=20+25+25=70(units)

Weighted average cost=1,575÷70=22.5($)

Cost of goods sold=22.5×55=1,237.5($)

Ending balance=1,575−1,237.5=337.5($)

EXHIBIT 4-4 shows the cost of goods sold and the inventory ending balance of Master Chef.

EXHIBIT 4-4 The Inventory Record of Master Chef under Average Cost Method

Inventory			
Beginning balance	20 units@ $20	$400	
Purchase 1	25 units@ $22	$550	Cost of goods sold 55 units@ $22.5 =$1,237.5
Purchase 2	25 units@ $25	$625	
Ending balance	15 units@ $22.5	$337.5	

4.5.3 First-in, First-out

FIFO refers to first-in, first-out. The FIFO method is a cost-assignment method and does not track the actual physical flow of individual items, except by coincidence. For identical units, it assigns the cost of the earliest acquired units (those that were "first-in") to cost of goods sold.

Let's take EXHIBIT 4-3 as an example:

Cost of goods sold=20×20+25×22+10×25=1,200($)

Ending balance=1,575−1,200=375($)

EXHIBIT 4-5 shows the inventory record of Master Chef under FIFO.

EXHIBIT 4-5 The Inventory Record of Master Chef under FIFO

Inventory					
Beginning balance	20 units@ $20	$400	20 units@ $20	$400	
Purchase 1	25 units@ $22	$550	25 units@ $22	$550	$1,200
Purchase 2	25 units@ $25	$625	10 units@ $25	$250	
Ending balance	15 units@ $25	$375			

4.5.4 Last-in, First-out

LIFO refers to last-in, first-out. Whereas FIFO associates the most recent costs with ending inventories, LIFO assigns the costs of the most recently acquired units to cost of goods sold.

Let's take EXHIBIT 4-3 as an example:

Cost of goods sold=25×25+25×22+5×20=1,275($)

Ending balance=1,575−1,275=300($)

EXHIBIT 4-6 shows the inventory record of Master Chef under LIFO.

EXHIBIT 4-6 The Inventory Record of Master Chef under LIFO

Inventory					
Beginning balance	20 units@ $20	$400	25 units@ $25	$625	
Purchase 1	25 units@ $22	$550	25 units@ $22	$550	$1,275
Purchase 2	25 units@ $25	$625	5 units@ $20	$100	
Ending balance	15 units@ $20	$300			

4.6 Summary of Inventory

The summary of inventory systems and inventory costing methods is shown in EXHIBIT 4-7.

EXHIBIT 4-7   Summary of Inventory

Question	Description	Method
Which inventory system should we use?	Can control inventory by visual inspection	Periodic system
	Cannot control inventory by visual inspection	Perpetual system
Which inventory costing method should we use?	Unique inventory items	Specific identification method
	Middle range approach for income tax and income	Average cost method
	Most current cost of ending inventory	FIFO
	Maximize income when cost is rising	
	Most current measure of cost of goods sold and net income	LIFO
	Minimize income tax when cost is rising	

4.7 Effects of Inventory Errors

Unfortunately, errors occasionally occur in accounting for inventory. In some cases, errors are caused by failure to count or price the inventory correctly. In other cases, errors occur because companies do not properly recognize the transfer of legal title to goods that are in transit. When errors occur, they affect both the income statement and the statement of financial position.

The ending inventory of one period automatically becomes the beginning inventory of the next period. Thus, inventory errors affect the computation of cost of goods sold and net income in two periods.

The cost of goods sold can be computed by using the formula in EXHIBIT 4-8.

EXHIBIT 4-8   Formula for Cost of Goods Sold

Beginning inventory + Cost of good purchased − Ending inventory = Cost of goods sold

If the beginning inventory is understated, the cost of goods sold will be understated. If the ending inventory is understated, the cost of goods sold will be overstated. EXHIBIT 4-9 shows the effects of inventory errors on the current year's income statement.

EXHIBIT 4-9 Effects of Inventory Errors on Current Year's Income Statement

When an Inventory Error:	Cost of Goods Sold Is:	Net Income Is:
Understates beginning inventory	Understated	Overstated
Overstates beginning inventory	Overstated	Understated
Understates ending inventory	Overstated	Understated
Overstates ending inventory	Understated	Overstated

4.8 Lower-of-Cost-or-Market Rule

Sometimes companies cannot easily sell obsolete or damaged inventory items at a price equal to or above their historical cost. In such a case, the historical cost overstates the value of the inventory. To avoid overstating the inventory, we use the **lower-of-cost-or-market (LCM) method**. LCM requires companies to compare the current market price of inventory with its historical cost derived under whichever inventory method the company has adopted and then report the lower of the two as the inventory value.

How companies measure current market price depends on whether they use IFRS or U.S. GAAP. Under IFRS, the market price is net realizable value — the net amount the company expects to receive when it sells the inventory. Under U.S. GAAP, it is usually current replacement cost — what it would cost to buy the inventory item today.

Suppose Master Chef bought some boxes of mineral water at $1,800 on November 13, 2022. On December 31, 2022, the market value of mineral water changed to $1,900. There is no need to make adjustment towards the change. The ending balance of inventory is still $1,800 on the balance sheet.

Suppose Master Chef bought some boxes of mineral water at $1,800 on November 13, 2022. On December 31, 2022, the market value of mineral water changed to $1,700.

November 13, 2022

Dr: Inventory   1,800
    Cr: Cash   1,800

December 31, 2022

Dr: Cost of goods sold   100
    Cr: Inventory   100

The ending balance of inventory should be changed to $1,700 on the balance sheet.

4.9 Inventory Turnover

The amount of inventory carried by a company has significant economic consequences, and inventory management is a double-edged sword that requires constant attention. On the one hand, management wants to have a great variety and quantity available so that customers have a wide selection and items are always in stock. But such a policy may incur high carrying costs (e.g., investment, storage, insurance, obsolescence, and damage). On the other hand, low inventory levels lead to stock-outs and lost sales. Common ratios used to manage and evaluate inventory levels are inventory turnover and a related measure, days in inventory.

Inventory turnover measures the number of times on average the inventory is sold during the period. Its purpose is to measure the liquidity of the inventory. The inventory turnover is computed by dividing cost of goods sold by the average inventory during the period. Unless seasonal factors are significant, average inventory can be computed from the beginning and ending inventory balances.

For example, Esprit Holdings reported in a recent annual report a beginning inventory of HK$3,209 million, an ending inventory of HK$3,254 million, and cost of goods sold for the year of HK$12,071 million. EXHIBIT 4-10 shows the inventory turnover formula and computation for Esprit Holdings.

EXHIBIT 4-10

Inventory Turnover Formula and Computation for Esprit Holdings (in Millions)

Cost of Goods Sold / Average Inventory = Inventory Turnover
HK$12,071 / {(HK$3,209 + HK$3,254) / 2} = 3.7 times

A variant of the inventory turnover is days in inventory. This measures the average number of days the inventory is held. It is calculated as 365 divided by the inventory turnover. For example, 365 devided by Esprit Holdings' inventory turnover of 3.7 times is approximately 99 days.

There are typical levels of inventory in every industry. Companies that are able to keep their inventory at lower levels and higher turnovers and still satisfy customers' needs are the most successful.

Core Words

Inventory	存货
Cost of goods sold	已销商品成本
Gross profit	毛利润
Periodic inventory system	实地盘存制
Perpetual inventory system	永续盘存制
Specific identification method	个别确认法
Average cost method	加权平均法
First-in, first-out	先进先出法
Last-in, first-out	后进先出法
Inventory turnover	存货周转率
Inventory errors	盘存差错

Extended Reading

1. 实地盘存制

　　实地盘存制又称定期盘存制，是指通过对期末库存存货的实物盘点，确定期末存货和当期销货成本的方法。实地盘存制不必通过账面连续记录得出期末存货，并假定除期末库存以外的存货均已售出，通过这种方法倒挤出销货成本。因此在实地盘存制下，日常经营中因销售而减少的存货不予记录，而只记录增加的存货。实地盘存制的优点是核算工作比较简单，工作量小。缺点是手续不够严密，不能通过账簿随时反映和监督各项财产物资的收、发、结存情况。当仓库管理中有多发少发、物资损毁、盗窃丢失等情况时，账面上均无反映，而全部隐藏于本期的发出存货当中，这往往会使得成本被高估，不利于存货的管理，也不利于监督检查。因此，实地盘存制只适用于数量大、价值低、收发频繁的存货，与永续盘存制相比安全性较差。

　　目前实地盘存制一般只适用于核算价值低、数量不稳定、损耗大的鲜活商品。

2. 永续盘存制

　　永续盘存制又叫账面盘存制，根据会计凭证在账簿中连续记录存货的增加和减少，并随时根据账簿记录结出账面结存数量。它是既登记购进数，又登记发出数，通过结账，能随时反映账面结存数的一种存货核算方法。永续盘存制的优点是可以通过存货的明细账记录，随时反映某一存货在一定会计期间内收入、发出和结存的详细情况，有利于加强对存货的管理和控制。同时可以通过盘点对实存数量进行核对，当发生损溢时，可以查明原因，及时纠正。该方法有利于防止库存的积压或不足。缺点是核算工作量较大。

永续盘存制适用于大部分企业。

3. 后进先出法

本章提到了后进先出法，这种方法在美国被大力推行。美国有将近一半的企业采用后进先出法，因为后进先出可以帮助企业在物价上涨(通货膨胀)期间合理避税。然而在我国，后进先出法是禁用的。

中国新会计准则取消后进先出法的主要原因在于，后进先出法将更早形成的成本留在企业存货中，将最近形成的价格分配给销售成本，这样长期累积下去的话，在通货膨胀期间会导致企业存货的公允价值被低估，降低各期的当期利润，而且这种方法会使得企业应交所得税减少。

后进先出法基于"后入库的先发出"这样一个存货流动假设，其基本特点是使所销售的存货按最近取得存货的成本与其实现的销售收入相配比。与先进先出法相比，一般来说，在物价持续上涨的情况下，后进先出法将会导致较高的销售成本、期末现金余额和较低的期末存货余额、销售毛利、所得税和净收益额，而当物价持续下跌时，结论恰好相反。因此，大部分企业一般只在预期存货的价格不断上涨时选择后进先出法，以达到递延所得税支出的目的，而当预期存货价格将持续下跌时，则通过会计政策变更将存货计价方法由后进先出法转为先进先出法。此外，一些企业之所以采用后进先出法，是因为其实物收发就是按"后进先出"的原则进行的，如总是保持基本存量的炼油、玻璃制造等行业。

4. 学习中不忘中国情怀

在马克思主义中国化的发展进程中，中华优秀传统文化日益成为中国特色社会主义先进文化的重要思想资源、中华民族共有精神家园的重要支撑、新时代鼓舞人民奋勇前进的强大精神力量。不忘本来才能开辟未来，善于继承才能更好创新。当前，如何继承和弘扬中华优秀传统文化，如何发挥中华传统文化的当代价值，如何努力实现中华优秀传统文化的创造性转化和创新性发展，使其真正发挥提升民众思想道德素养、提高社会思想道德水平的巨大功能，是做好马克思主义理论与现实研究的重大课题。深入挖掘和发挥中华优秀传统文化对思想政治教育的资源性支持，继承和弘扬中国传统文化的精髓与做好思想政治教育工作，是我们党在思想政治教育领域上的重大理论创新和重大战略任务。

Exercises

1. Which of the following statements about the inventory system is wrong? (   )

    A. In perpetual inventory system, we don't need to count the inventory physically.

    B. Perpetual inventory system can be used for all types of goods.

    C. Perpetual inventory system keeps a running record of inventory.

    D. Perpetual inventory system is better than periodic inventory system.

2. Which item should be added to recognize the cost of purchased inventory? (   )

    A. Fright-in.   B. Purchase return.

    C. Purchase allowance.   D. Purchase discount.

3. Which inventory costing method is not allowed to use in China? (   )

    A. Specific identification. B. Average cost.

    C. FIFO.   D. LIFO.

4. Which of the following statements about specific identification method is true? (   )

    A. It can lead to maximum of net income.

    B. It can lead to highest ending inventory.

    C. It is suitable for inventory with high value and low quantity.

    D. It is the most common inventory costing method.

5. The beginning inventory is $18,000, and newly purchase is $50,000. The net sales are $60,000. The gross profit rate of the entity is 35%. What is the ending balance of inventory? (   )

    A. $8,000.   B. $39,000.

    C. $29,000.   D. $50,000.

6. Which of the following can lead to the most current cost of ending inventory? (   )

    A. Specific identification. B. FIFO.

    C. LIFO.   D. Average cost.

7. Which of the following can lead to the most current measure of cost of goods sold and net income? (   )

    A. Specific identification. B. FIFO.

    C. LIFO.   D. Average cost.

Inventory and Cost of Goods Sold — Chapter 4

8. Which of the following can maximize the reported income when the market price is rising? (   )

   A. Specific identification.   B. FIFO.
   C. LIFO.   D. Average cost.

9. Which of the following can minimize the income tax when the market price is rising? (   )

   A. Specific identification.   B. FIFO.
   C. LIFO.   D. Average cost.

10. In lower-of-cost-or-market principle, "market" means (   ).

    A. original cost   B. present value
    C. replacement cost   D. net realizable value

11. Carlos Cookware had beginning inventory of €80,000, ending inventory of €110,000, cost of goods sold of €285,000, and sales of €475,000. Carlos' days in inventory was (   ).

    A. 73 days   B. 121.7 days
    C. 102.5 days   D. 84.5 days

12. Cost of goods available for sale consists of two elements: beginning inventory and (   ).

    A. ending inventory   B. cost of goods purchased
    C. cost of goods sold   D. all of the answers are correct

13. In periods of rising prices, average cost method will produce (   ).

    A. higher net income than FIFO

    B. the same net income as FIFO

    C. lower net income than FIFO

    D. net income equal to the specific identification method

14. Factors that affect the selection of an inventory costing method do not include (   ).

    A. tax effects

    B. statement of financial position effects

    C. income statement effects

    D. perpetual vs. periodic inventory system

15. Atlantis Aquarium's ending inventory is understated NT$122,000. The effects of this error on the current year's cost of goods sold and net income, respectively, are (   ).

    A. understated, overstated   B. overstated, understated
    C. overstated, overstated   D. understated, understated

16. AAA Company uses the periodic inventory system to manage its inventory. AAA Company's beginning inventory is 100, @$75. On January 2, AAA bought 200 units @$80;

on January 15, AAA bought 90 units @$85; on January 15, AAA bought 240 units @$90. The selling price is $135 each, and there are 130 units left at the end of the period.

Calculate the cost of goods sold and the gross profit by using the average cost method, FIFO, and LIFO respectively.

17. BBB Company uses the perpetual inventory system to manage its inventory, and BBB Company's inventory is shown in the following exhibit.

		Inventory	
Beginning balance	20 units@ $20	$400	
Purchase 1	25 units@ $22	$550	Cost of goods sold 85 units@?
Purchase 2	25 units@ $25	$625	
Purchase 3	30 units@ $30	$900	
Ending balance	15 units@?		

Calculate the cost of goods sold and the ending balance of the inventory by using the average cost method, FIFO, and LIFO respectively.

Chapter 5
Investment

Spotlight

In general, to invest is to allocate money or sometimes another resource in the expectation of some benefits in the future—for example, investment in durable goods, in real estate by the service industry, in factories for manufacturing, in product development, and in research and development. However, this chapter focuses specifically on investment in financial assets.

A number of companies make investment decisions in debt or share markets for generating earnings. Moreover, some of them purchase other companies' shares for various strategic considerations depending on the percentage of shares they are willing to hold.

Vanky Corporation is an air conditioning company. It has more sales in summer and fall than in spring and winter. At the end of October of 2022 when the fall was over, Vanky had cash on hand that was temporarily idle until the start of next summer. It was planning to invest the excess funds in debt or share to earn a greater return than it would get by just holding the excess funds in the bank. After analyzing the bond and share markets, Vanky determined to acquire Wesper bonds and Antac Ltd. shares, and tended to sell them in the near future. How do you account for the investment activities? Did Vanky gain or lose money on these two investments?

Text

5.1 Debt Investments

Debt investments are investments in bonds of the government, banks, and companies. Debt investments are classified into trading securities and held-for-colleciton securities.

5.1.1 Accounting for Acquisition of Bonds

At the time of acquisition, the debt investment is recorded at cost.

Vanky Corporation acquired 50 Wesper 5%, 10-year, $2,000 bonds on January 1, 2022, at a cost of $100,000. The journal entry is:

January 1, 2022

   Dr: Debt investments   100,000

      Cr: Cash   100,000

5.1.2 Accounting for Receipt of Bond Interest

Wesper pays bond interest on January 1 annually. The adjusting journal entry based on accrual basis on December 31, 2022 is:

December 31, 2022

   Dr: Interest receivable   5,000

      Cr: Interest revenue   5,000

Vanky received the bond interest on January 1, 2023, the entry was recorded as:

January 1, 2023

   Dr: Cash   5,000

      Cr: Interest receivable   5,000

5.1.3 Accounting for Sale of Bonds

At the time of selling the bonds, the debt investments account should be credited at cost. In addition, if the net sales proceeds of the bonds differ from the cost, a gain or loss needs to be recognized.

Vanky sold all bonds it was holding on January 1, 2023, and received $110,000 net sales proceeds after the receipt of the interest due. In this case, Vanky realized a gain of $10,000, benefiting from the net sales proceeds exceeding the cost. The journal entry to record the sales transaction is:

January 1, 2023

   Dr: Cash   110,000

      Cr: Debt investments   100,000

         Gain on sale of debt investments   10,000

5.2 Share Investments

Share investments are investments in shares of other companies. The proportion of ordinary shares held by an investor determines the extent of its influence over the investee's operating and financial affairs, which directly results in the methods applied for accounting.

Share investments are classified into trading securities and non-trading securities.

5.2.1 Less than 20% Ownership

Holdings of less than 20% means that the investor has an insignificant influence on the investee. The **cost method** is applied to account for the share investments of less than 20%.

- **Accounting for Acquisition of Shares**

At the time of acquisition, the share investment is recorded at cost.

Vanky Corporation purchased 2,000 shares at the price of $400 per share, holding 10% of the ordinary shares of Antac Ltd. on January 1, 2022. The journal entry is:

January 1, 2022

Dr: Share investments	800,000
Cr: Cash	800,000

- **Accounting for Receipt of Dividends**

Under the cost method, dividend revenue is only recognized at the time of receiving cash dividends. Thus, unlike the recording of bond interests, adjusting entries are not required to accrue dividends.

Vanky received the cash dividends of $15 per share on December 31, 2022. The journal entry of the receipt of dividends is:

December 31, 2022

Dr: Cash	30,000
Cr: Dividend revenue	30,000

- **Accounting for Sale of Shares**

At the time of selling the shares, the share investments account should be credited at cost. In addition, if the net sales proceeds of the shares differ from the cost, a gain or loss needs to be recognized.

Vanky sold all shares it was holding on January 1, 2023, and received $750,000 net sales proceeds. In this case, Vanky had to incur a loss of $50,000, resulting from the net sales proceeds below the cost. The entry to record the sales transaction is:

January 1, 2023

Dr: Cash	750,000
Loss on sale of share investments	50,000
Cr: Share investments	800,000

5.2.2 Between 20% and 50% Ownership

When a company is holding 20% - 50% of ordinary shares of another company, it means that the investor has a significant influence but no control over the investee. The **equity method** is applied to account for the share investments of **between 20% and 50%.**

- **Accounting for Acquisition of Shares**

At the time of acquisition, the share investment is recorded at cost.

Vanky Corporation acquired 40% of the ordinary shares of Charty Ltd. for $150,000 on January 1, 2022. The journal entry is:

January 1, 2022

Dr: Share investments	150,000	
Cr: Cash		150,000

- **Accounting for Receipt of Dividends**

Under the equity method, the investor adjusts the share investments account annually in order to show its equity in the investee.

Charty Ltd. reported a net income of $200,000 in the year of 2022, declared and paid $80,000 of cash dividends to all investors. The journal entries of the receipt of dividends are:

December 31, 2022

Dr: Share investments	80,000	
Cr: Revenue from share investments		80,000

Vanky debited the share investments account and credited revenue for its share of the net income of Charty Ltd.

Dr: Cash	32,000	
Cr: Share investments		32,000

Vanky credited the share investments account for the amount of dividends received.

5.2.3 More than 50% Ownership

When an investor is holding more than 50% of ordinary shares of an investee, the investor can be called a parent company, and the investee can be called a subsidiary company. The investor (parent company) has a controlling interest in the investee (subsidiary company). Under such condition of share ownership, companies prepare **consolidated financial statements** as well as their own individual financial statements.

5.3 Short-term Investments and Long-term Investments

5.3.1 Short-term Investments

Short-term investments are also called **marketable securities**. They are investments that a company plans to hold for one year or less. They allow the company to invest cash for a short period of time and earn a return when the cash is needed. Short-term investments are the next-most-liquid asset after cash.

The most typical short-term investments are **trading securities** which can be both debt investments and share investments. Non-trading securities and held-for-collection securities can be short-term in some circumstances.

- **Trading Securities**

As is indicated above, trading securities and held-for-collection securities are two categories of debt investments. **Trading securities** are held for sale in the near future. Companies can generate earnings due to the price differences between the fair value and the cost. Trading securities are reported on the balance sheet at their current **fair value**, because the fair value keeps fluctuating in the securities market. At the end of the year, the investor needs to adjust the trading securities to their current fair value. The difference between the cost of trading securities and their fair value is called **unrealized gains or losses**. The word "unrealized" is used because the investor has not sold the securities yet.

(1) Unrealized Gain. Gain because the fair value is greater than the cost of the investment.

Suppose that the fair value of Wesper bonds increased to $108,000 on December 31, 2022. The adjusting entry is:

December 31, 2022

 Dr: Fair value adjustment-trading   8,000
  Cr: Unrealized gain or loss-income   8,000

(2) Unrealized Loss. Loss because the fair value is less than the cost of the investment.

Suppose that the fair value of Wesper bonds decreased to $98,000 on December 31, 2022. The adjusting entry is:

December 31, 2022

 Dr: Unrealized gain or loss-income   2,000
  Cr: Fair value adjustment-trading   2,000

5.3.2 Long-term Investments

Investments that are not short-term are listed as **long-term investments**. They are investments that a company plans to hold for more than one year. Long-term investments are less liquid than current assets but more liquid than property, plant, and equipment.

Long-term investments include **non-trading securities** (share investments only) and **held-for-collection securities** (debt investments only), and these two investments can also be short-term investments in some circumstances. The most typical long-term investments are non-trading securities.

- **Non-trading Securities**

As is indicated above, trading securities and non-trading securities are two categories of share investments. **Non-trading securities** are the share investments that are not for trading. They could be for strategic considerations. They are classified as currents if the business expects to sell them in one year, or else they are classified as non-current assets.

Non-trading securities are accounted for at their fair value, because the company expects to sell the investments at their fair prices. The cost is used only as the initial amount for recording the investments. Non-trading securities are reported on the balance sheet at their current fair value, which will result in a difference between the fair value and the cost, so an adjusting entry is necessary to record the difference.

(1) Unrealized Gain. Gain because the fair value is greater than the cost of the investment.

Suppose that Vanky was not about to sell Antac Ltd. shares due to strategic reasons, and the fair value of the holding shares increased to $830,000 on December 31, 2022. The adjusting entry is:

December 31, 2022

 Dr: Fair value adjustment-non-trading   30,000
  Cr: Unrealized gain or loss-equity   30,000

(2) Unrealized Loss. Loss because the fair value is less than the cost of the investment.

Suppose that Vanky didn't sell Antac Ltd. shares, and the fair value of the holding shares decreased to $715,000 on December 31, 2022. The adjusting entry is:

December 31, 2022

 Dr: Unrealized gain or loss-equity   85,000
  Cr: Fair value adjustment-non-trading   85,000

- **Held-for-collection Securities**

Held-for-collection securities are the debt investments that a business intends to hold until their maturity. They are reported at **amortized cost** at the end of the financial period. Amortized cost equals the initial cost less repayments, and then minus or plus the accumulated amortization of premiums or discounts.

Core Words

Debt investments	债券投资
Share investments	股份投资
Cost method	成本法
Equity method	权益法
Parent company	母公司
Subsidiary company	子公司
Consolidated financial statements	合并财务报表
Short-term investments	短期投资
Long-term investments	长期投资
Trading securities	交易性金融资产
Non-trading securities	非交易性金融资产
Held-for-colletion securities	持有至到期投资
Unrealized gain	或有利润(未实现收益)
Unrealized loss	或有损失(未实现损失)
Fair value	公允价值
Amortized cost	摊余成本

Extended Reading

1. 交易性金融资产

交易性金融资产是指企业以赚差价为目的而持有，准备近期内出售的债券投资、股票投资和基金投资。交易性金融资产是2007年新增的会计科目，主要是为了适应股票、债券、基金等的市场交易。交易性金融资产取代了原来的短期投资，二者反映的内容相似但又有所不同。而在美国，依然使用短期投资科目对交易性金融资产进行核算。

交易性金融资产具有如下特点：

(1) 企业持有的目的是短期性的，即在初次确认时就确认其持有目的是短期获利。此处所指的短期通常不超过一年(包括一年)。

(2) 交易性金融资产具有活跃市场，公允价值能够通过活跃市场获取。

(3) 交易性金融资产持有期间不计提资产减值损失。

(4) 交易性金融资产以公允价值计量且其变动计入当期损益。

2. 非交易性金融资产

非交易性金融资产是指不具备交易性的金融资产，如果一项金融资产不是用于投资和套期保值的，就不符合交易性金融资产的条件，因而属于非交易性金融资产。

3. 持有至到期投资

持有至到期投资是指企业打算并且能够持有至到期的债权证券。所有持有至到期投资在购入时都要以成本入账，利息收入则要在赚得时入账。 2017年，财政部发布了《企业会计准则第22号——金融工具确认和计量》，执行企业会计准则的企业应当不再使用"持有至到期投资"科目，而将其替换成"债权投资"。

4. 我国资本市场的发展与成就

1978年，改革开放被定为我国的基本国策，此后经济建设成为国家发展的基本任务。为了适应企业发展的需求和促进我国国有企业股份制改革的顺利进行，我国资本市场开始萌芽和发展。1990年，作为一种试验性的经济体制改革，中国资本市场被正式建立。同年，上海证券交易所(以下简称上交所)和深圳证券交易所(以下简称深交所)正式成立和营业，我国证券交易市场自此正式建立。1992年，一些国有企业成功完成了股份制改革，开始在证券市场上市，我国资本市场初现雏形。为了更有效地对证券市场形成监督和约束，我国成立了国务院证券管理委员会和证监会。我国监管机构在成立之初发布了一系列规章制度，为规范上市公司的管理起到了重要作用。在这一时期，证监会先后颁布了规范股票发行和交易、规范上市公司信息披露行为和禁止欺诈的相关管理条例，规范了我国证券市场的运行。此后，《公司法》于1994年开始正式实施，针对公司的设立、组织、股份发行与交易、法人治理机构等活动做出了详细的规定和约束，进一步增强了我国企业经营的合规性。除了上市公司，这一时期我国从事证券投资的证券公司和基金公司也得到了有效的规范和管理。1998年，伴随着《证券法》的颁布和实施，我国资本市场正式在法律层面上得到了承认。我国资本市场的法律体系、信息披露规则和会计规则等日益完善，资本市场的监管体制和执法体系逐步建立和健全，稽查执法工作不断加强。为了适应资本市场的发展需要，我国证券市场的审批制度也正式退出了历史舞台，我国资本市场开始了针对股票发行制度的探索。2001年，通道制的股票发行制度被采纳和实施。2003年，保荐制开始实施。

　　2004年，国务院发文坚定了发展我国资本市场的信念，同时给出了我国资本市场进一步发展的规划蓝图，此举很大程度上稳定了我国金融市场的发展。此后，2005年到2008年之间，我国资本市场开展并完成了上市公司的股权分置改革的进程，证券市场上的流通股和非流通股之间不再存在差异，这一运行机制更加符合市场化规律，股东之间的权益也得到了有效的平衡。创业板正式成立于2009年，证监会正式宣告了创业板的建立。创业板创建之后，很快就迎来了多次快速扩容，并于2014年开始实施做市商制度，于2016年结束试运行，创业板正式成为一个面向全国的股转系统。2020年，创业板成为深交所的注册制试点，这一个改革标志着注册制正式进入存量板块。创业板也开启了我国资本市场的多层次发展的序幕。继创业板之后，我国资本市场又迎来了科创板，进一步丰富了我国资本市场多层次发展的需要。2021年是我国资本市场建立的第30年，截至2021年2月18日，我国的上市公司数量已经超过4000家，相较于我国资本市场成立之初，上市公司数量增长了五百多倍。①

Exercises

1. A company bought the shares of B company on March 1, 2022 at $85,000. A company identified the investment as trading securities. On December 31, 2022, the shares were valued at $83,000. What is the balance of this investment on the balance sheet? (　　)

　　A. $85,000.　　　　　　　　　　　　B. $83,000.

　　C. $2,000 realized loss.　　　　　　　 D. $2,000 unrealized loss.

2. A company bought the shares of B company on March 1, 2022 for $85,000. A company identified the investment as trading securities. On December 31, 2022, the shares were valued at $83,000. What should appear on the income statement? (　　)

　　A. $85,000.　　　　　　　　　　　　B. $83,000.

---

　　① 资料来源：我国资本市场的发展史 [EB/OL]. https://baijiahao.baidu.com/s?id=1740395248808107718&wfr=spider&for=pc, 2022-08-06.

C. $2,000 realized loss.   D. $2,000 unrealized loss.

3. Which of the following statements about debt investments is true? (   )

   A. Debt investments should be initially recorded at amortized cost.

   B. Non-trading securities belong to debt investments.

   C. Debt investments are initially recorded at cost.

   D. Debt investments are long-term investments.

4. A company has a significant influence but no control over the investee when it is holding (   ).

   A. 20% - 50% of ordinary shares of another company

   B. less than 20% of ordinary shares of another company

   C. more than 50% of ordinary shares of another company

   D. 100% of ordinary shares of another company

5. The cost method is applied to account for the share investments of (   ).

   A. between 20% and 50%

   B. less than 20%

   C. more than 50%

   D. 100%

6. The purpose of which short-term investment is to hold it for a short time and then sell it for more than its cost? (   )

   A. Trading securities.

   B. Non-trading securities.

   C. Held-for-collection securities.

   D. Stock.

7. Select all the answers that are correct: When an investor is holding 65% of the ordinary shares of an investee, what financial statements are supposed to be prepared? (   )

   A. Consolidated financial statements.

   B. Financial statements for the parent company.

   C. Financial statements for the subsidiary company.

   D. None of the above.

8. AAA Corporation wanted to get into the electronics business, so it purchased 2,000 shares at the price of $500 per share, holding 15% of the ordinary shares of LOP Ltd. on January 1, 2022. AAA recognized the investment as non-trading securities. AAA received the cash dividends of $20 per share on December 31, 2022. The fair value of the shares

held by AAA turned to $1,050,000 on December 31, 2022.

Please make journal entries of the above transactions.

(1) January 1, 2022

(2) December 31, 2022

Chapter 6

Plant Assets, Natural Resources, and Intangible Assets

Spotlight

The accounting for non-current assets has important implications for a company's reported results. Tangible assets and intangibles are important parts of the long-term assets of an enterprise, especially to production corporations. For example, Blue Fly Corporations is a food production factory. This company has a lot of large production equipment and some plants. The balance sheet of Blue Fly Corporation is shown in EXHIBIT 6-1.

EXHIBIT 6-1   The Balance Sheet of Blue Fly Corporation

Balance Sheet
December 31, 2022

(Amounts in thousands)		
Assets		
Current assets		proportion
Cash and cash equivalents	211	5%
Short-term investments	145	3%
Accounts receivable	245	6%
Inventories	622	14%
Other current assets	<u>43</u>	1%
Total current assets	1,266	29%
Long-term investments	225	5%
Property, plant, and equipment, net	2,288	53%
Intangible assets	399	9%
Other assets	<u>165</u>	4%
Total assets	<u>4,343</u>	100%

Through the report we can find out that the long-term assets accounted for a significant proportion of the total assets. It's an important issue for the Blue Fly Corporation to manage the long-term assets. How do we make initial confirmation of the long-term assets? Is the book value of the long-term assets invariable? In this chapter, we will focus on accounting for tangible assets and intangible assets.

Chapter 6 Plant Assets, Natural Resources, and Intangible Assets

Text

6.1 Plant Assets

Plant assets are resources that have three characteristics. They have a physical substance (a definite size and shape), are used in the operations of a business, and are not intended for sale to customers. They are also called **property, plant, and equipment**; or **fixed assets**. These assets are expected to be of use to the company for a number of years. Except for land, plant assets decline in service potential over their useful lives.

6.1.1　Land

Companies often use their land as a site for a manufacturing plant or an office building. The cost of land includes (1) the purchase price, (2) closing costs such as title and attorneys' fees, (3) real estate brokers' commissions, and (4) accrued property taxes and other liens assumed by the purchaser.

Sometimes, the land has a building on it that must be removed before construction of a new building. In this case, the company debits to the land account all the demolition and removal costs, less any proceeds from salvaged materials.

6.1.2　Land Improvements

Land improvements are structural additions with limited lives that are made to land. Examples are paving, fencing, and lighting. The cost of land improvements includes all the expenditures necessary to make the improvements ready for their intended use. Land improvements have limited useful lives. Even when well-maintained, they will eventually be replaced. As a result, companies expense (depreciate) the cost of land improvements over their useful lives.

6.1.3　Buildings

- **Constructed Buildings**

The cost of constructing a building includes architectural fees, building permits, constructor charges, interest on money borrowed from the bank, and payments for material, labor, and overhead.

- **Purchased Buildings**

The cost of a purchased building includes the purchase price, brokerage commission, taxes, and all the expenditures to repair and renovate the building for its intended purpose.

6.1.4 Machinery and Equipment

The cost of equipment includes its purchase price (less any discounts), transportation fee, commission fee, installation cost, and any other expenditures incurred for bringing the asset to the expected condition for use.

The acquisition cost of equipment of Blue Fly Corporation is shown in EXHIBIT 6-2.

EXHIBIT 6-2 Acquisition Cost of Equipment

Items	Dollars
Invoice price, gross	200,000
Cash discount, 2%	(4,000)
Invoice price, net	196,000
Transportation cost	2,000
Installation cost	5,000
Repair cost prior to use	2,200
Commissions	4,000
Total acquisition cost	209,200

6.2 Capitalized Expenditures and Immediate Expenses

When a company spends money on a plant asset, it must decide whether to record it as an asset or an expense.

Costs that increase the asset's capacity or extend its useful life are called **capitalized expenditures**, which means the costs are added to an asset account instead of recorded as an expense, for example, an overhaul for a machine.

Costs that do not extend the asset's capacity or its useful life, but just maintain normal use of the asset or restore it to working order, are recorded as **expenses**, for example, a repair for a machine.

6.3 Account for Depreciation of Plant Assets

6.3.1 Depreciation

Depreciation is the process of allocating to expense the cost of a plant asset over its useful (service) life in a rational and systematic manner. Cost allocation enables companies to properly match expenses with revenues in accordance with the expense recognition principle. Fixed assets need to be depreciated regularly after they are recorded in the accounts. All kinds of plant assets need to be depreciated, except land. Plant assets are reported on the balance sheet at book value.

Book value=Historical cost – Accumulated depreciation

The journal entry for depreciation is:

Dr: Depreciation expense ×××
　　Cr: Accumulated depreciation ×××

Depreciation expense is recorded on the income statement, and accumulated depreciation is recorded on the balance sheet.

6.3.2　Factors in Computing Depreciation

How can we measure depreciation?

There are three elements about depreciation:

♦ Historical cost.
♦ Estimated useful life.
♦ Estimated residual value.

6.3.3　Depreciation Method

Blue Fly Corporation bought a machine at $55,000 on January 1, 2018, and the estimated useful life was 5 years or 100,000 working units. The estimated residual value was $5,000.

There are three main methods to calculate depreciation. Each method is acceptable under IFRS. The management selects the method which is believed to be appropriate. The objective is to select the method that best measures an asset's contribution to revenue over its useful life. Once a company chooses a method, it should apply it consistently over the useful life of the asset. Consistency enhances the comparability of financial statements. Depreciation affects the statement of financial position through accumulated depreciation and the income statement through depreciation expense.

● **Straight-line Depreciation Method**

Straight-line depreciation method spreads the depreciable value evenly over the useful life of an asset. Depreciable cost is divided by useful life in years to determine the annual depreciation expense.

$$\text{Depreciation per year} = \frac{\text{Cost} - \text{Residual value}}{\text{Years of useful life}}$$

$$\text{Depreciation per year} = \frac{\$55,000 - \$5,000}{5} = \$10,000$$

The calculations are shown in EXHIBIT 6-3.

EXHIBIT 6-3 Blue Fly Corporation: Straight-line Depreciation Method

	Annual depreciation($)	Accumulated depreciation($)	Book value($)
Jan.1, 2018			55,000
Dec.31, 2018	10,000	10,000	45,000
Dec.31, 2019	10,000	20,000	35,000
Dec.31, 2020	10,000	30,000	25,000
Dec.31, 2021	10,000	40,000	15,000
Dec.31, 2022	10,000	50,000	5,000 (residual value)

- **Double-declining-balance Depreciation Method**

Double-declining-balance(DDB) depreciation method is an accelerated depreciation method. There are four steps to calculate the depreciation expense.

First, compute the straight-line depreciation rate. The depreciation rate is simply 100% divided by the useful life of an asset.

Second, multiply the straight-line depreciation rate by 2 to calculate the DDB rate.

Third, multiply the DDB rate by the book value of an asset.

Fourth, determine the final year's depreciation amount.

The calculations are shown in EXHIBIT 6-4.

EXHIBIT 6-4 Blue Fly Corporation: Double-Declining-Balance Depreciation Method

	DDB rate	Annual depreciation($)	Accumulateddepreciation($)	Bookvalue($)
Jan.1, 2018	40%			55,000
Dec.31, 2018	40%	22,000	22,000	33,000
Dec.31, 2019	40%	13,200	35,200	19,800
Dec.31, 2020	40%	7,920	43,120	11,880
Dec.31, 2021	40%	4,752	47,672	7,128
Dec.31, 2022	40%	2,128*	50,000	5,000

Plant Assets, Natural Resources, and Intangible Assets

The DDB method is different from the other methods in two aspects:

First, residual value is ignored initially during the first year. Depreciation is computed in full cost of an asset.

Second, depreciation expense in the final year is the "plug" amount needed to reduce the asset's book value to the residual amount.

- **Units-of-production Depreciation Method**

Sometimes the useful life of an asset does not indicate the actual use of the asset, for example, Blue Fly Corporation could depreciate the depreciation of its machine on basis of the actual workload. Suppose the machine's useful life is 100,000 hours.

$$\text{Depreciation per unit} = \frac{\text{Cost} - \text{Residual value}}{\text{Unit of service}}$$

$$\text{Depreciation per unit} = \frac{\$55,000 - \$5,000}{100,000} = \$0.5 \text{ per working unit}$$

If the machine works 6,000 hours in one year, the depreciation expenses should be:

$$\$0.5 \times 6,000 = \$3,000$$

6.4 Revaluation of Plant Assets

IFRS allows companies to revalue plant assets to their fair value at the reporting date. Companies that choose to use the revaluation framework must follow revaluation procedures. If revaluation is used, it must be applied to all assets in a class of assets. Assets that are experiencing rapid price changes must be revalued on an annual basis. Otherwise, less frequent revaluation is acceptable.

6.4.1 Situation of Gain

To illustrate asset revaluation accounting, assume that Blue Fly Corporation applied revaluation to a piece of equipment purchased on January 1, 2022, at $1,000,000. The equipment has a useful life of 5 years and no residual value. On December 31, 2022, Pernice made the following journal entry to record depreciation expense in 2022. Assume that straight-line depreciation method was used.

  Dr: Depreciation expense   200,000
    Cr: Accumulated depreciation   200,000

After this entry, this equipment had a carrying amount of $800,000 ($1,000,000−$200,000).

At the end of 2022, independent appraisers determined that the asset had a fair value of $850,000. To report the equipment at its fair value of $850,000 on December 31, 2022, Blue Fly eliminated the accumulated depreciation—equipment account, reduced the equipment to its fair value of $850,000, and recorded **revaluation surplus** of $50,000. The entry to record the revaluation is as follows.

  Dr: Accumulated depreciation—equipment   200,000
    Cr: Equipment   150,000
      Revaluation surplus   50,000

Thus, accounting follows a two-step process. First, record depreciation based on the cost basis. As a result, depreciation expense is reported on the income statement. Second, record the revaluation. This is done by eliminating any accumulated depreciation, adjusting the recorded value of the equipment to its fair value, and crediting the revaluation surplus account. Revaluation surplus is an example of an item reported as **other comprehensive income**.

In this example, the revaluation surplus is $50,000, which is the difference between the fair value of $850,000 and the book value of $800,000. Blue Fly Corporation reported the following information in its statement of financial position at the end of 2022 as shown in EXHIBIT 6-5.

EXHIBIT 6-5 Calculation of Revaluation Surplus

Items	Dollars
Equipment	$850,000 ($1,000,000 − $150,000)
Accumulated depreciation—equipment	$0
net	$850,000
Revaluation surplus (equity)	$50,000

Blue Fly Corporation reported depreciation expense of $200,000 in the income statement and $50,000 in other comprehensive income. As indicated, $850,000 became the new basis of the asset.

6.4.2 Situation of Loss

Assume again that Blue Fly's equipment has a carrying amount of $800,000. However, at the end of 2022, independent appraisers determined that the asset had a fair value of $775,000, which resulted in an **impairment loss** of $25,000 ($800,000−$775,000). To record the equipment at its fair value and to record this loss, the accountant first eliminated the balance in the accumulated depreciation—equipment account of $200,000. Next, it reduced the equipment account by $225,000 to report the equipment at $775,000 ($1,000,000−$225,000).

The entry to record the equipment and report the impairment loss is as follows:

Dr: Accumulated depreciation—equipment	200,000	
Impairment loss	25,000	
Cr: Equipment		225,000

The impairment loss of $25,000 reduced the net income.

6.5 Disposal of Plant Assets

Companies dispose of plant assets that are no longer useful to them. No matter what disposal method is used, the company must determine the book value of the plant asset at the disposal date to determine the gain or loss.

6.5.1 Retirement of Plant Assets

To illustrate the retirement of plant assets, assume that Blue Fly Corporation retires its computer printers, which cost $18,000. The accumulated depreciation on these printers is $14,000. In this case, the equipment retires before it is fully depreciated, and no cash is received for scrap or residual value, so a loss on disposal occurs. The entry to record this retirement is as follows.

Dr: Accumulated depreciation—equipment	14,000	
Loss on disposal of plant assets	4,000	
Cr: Equipment		18,000

Companies report a loss on disposal of plant assets in the "other income and expense" section of the income statement.

What happens if a fully depreciated plant asset is still useful to the company? In this case, the asset and its accumulated depreciation continue to be reported on the statement of financial position, without further depreciation adjustment, until the company retires the asset and informs the financial statement reader that the asset is not in use. Once an asset is fully depreciated, no additional depreciation should be taken, even if the asset is still being used. In no situation can the accumulated depreciation on a plant asset exceed its cost.

6.5.2 Sale of Plant Assets

Another disposal method is disposal by sale, in which the company compares the book value of the asset with the proceeds received from the sale. If the proceeds of the sale exceed the book value of the plant asset, a **gain on disposal** occurs. If the proceeds of the sale are less than the book value of the plant asset sold, a **loss on disposal** occurs.

- **Gain on Sale**

To illustrate a gain on sale of plant assets, assume that on July 1, 2022, Blue Fly Corporation sold its office furniture for $16,000 cash. The office furniture originally cost $60,000. As of July 1, 2022, it had accumulated depreciation of $49,000. The accountant recorded the sale and the gain on disposal of the plant asset as follows.

July 1	Dr: Cash	16,000
	Accumulated depreciation—equipment	49,000
	Cr: Equipment	60,000
	Gain on disposal of plant assets	5,000

- **Loss on Sale**

Assume that instead of selling the office furniture for $16,000, Blue Fly Corporation sold it for $9,000. The accountant recorded the sale and the loss on disposal of the plant asset as follows.

July 1	Dr: Cash	9,000
	Accumulated depreciation—equipment	49,000
	Loss on disposal of plant assets	2,000
	Cr: Equipment	60,000

Companies report a gain or a loss on disposal of plant assets in the "other income and expense" section of the income statement.

6.6 Natural Resources and Depletion

6.6.1 Natural Resources

Common **natural resources** consist of standing timber and resources extracted from the ground, such as oil, gas, and minerals. On a statement of financial position, natural resources may be described more specifically as timberlands, mineral deposits, oil reserves, and so on. Standing timber is considered a **biological asset** under IFRS. In the years before they are harvested, the recorded value of biological assets is adjusted to their fair value each period.

IFRS defines extractive industries as those businesses involved in finding and removing natural resources located in or near the earth's crust. The acquisition cost of an extractable natural resource is the price needed to acquire the resource and prepare it for its intended use. For an already-discovered resource, such as an existing coal mine, the cost is the price paid for

Plant Assets, Natural Resources, and Intangible Assets

the property.

6.6.2 Depletion

The allocation of the cost of natural resources in a rational and systematic manner over the resource's useful life is called **depletion**. Companies generally use the units-of-activity method to compute depletion. The reason is that depletion generally is a function of the units extracted during the year. Under the units-of-production method, companies divide the total cost of the natural resource minus residual value by the number of units estimated to be in the resource. The result is the depletion cost per unit. To compute depletion, the cost per unit is then multiplied by the number of units extracted.

$$\frac{\text{Total cost} - \text{Residual value}}{\text{Total estimated units available}} = \text{Depletion cost per unit}$$

6.7 Intangible Assets

Intangible assets are long-lived assets with no physical form. Intangibles are valuable because they carry special rights from patent, copyrights, trademarks, franchises, and goodwill. Like buildings and equipment, an intangible asset is recorded at its acquisition cost. Intangibles are the most valuable assets of high-tech companies and those depending on research and development.

6.7.1 Category of the Intangible Assets

- **Patents**

Patents are granted by federal government that gives the holder the exclusive right for 20 years to produce and sell an invention. The invention may be a product or a process. Like any other asset, a patent may be purchased.

Suppose that Blue Fly Corporation bought a patent on March 1, 2022 and paid cash of $100,000. The journal entry for this transaction is:

    Dr: Patent   100,000

        Cr: Cash   100,000

- **Copyrights**

Copyrights are exclusive rights to reproduce and sell a book, musical composition, film, software program, and other forms of art. Issued by American federal government, copyrights extend 70 years beyond the owners' life. The cost of obtaining a copyright from the government is low, but a company may pay large sum to purchase an existing copyright from the owner.

Suppose that Blue Fly Corporation bought a copyright from a software company on March 1, 2022 and paid cash of $100,000. The journal entry for this transaction is:

Dr: Copyright   100,000
    Cr: Cash   100,000

- **Trademarks**

Trademarks are also called **brand names**. A trademark is a distinctive identification of a product or service. It is a special name, sign, or word that is marked on a product to show that it is made by a particular company, and cannot be used by any other companies.

A trademark may have a definite useful life set by contract. We should amortize this trademark's cost over its useful life. A trademark or a brand name may also have an indefinite life. Trademarks with indefinite life do not need to be amortized.

- **Franchises**

Franchises are privileges granted by a private business or a government to sell a product or service in accordance with specified conditions. It is a permission given by a company to someone who wants to sell its goods or services. The useful lives of many franchises are indefinite, and therefore, are not amortized.

- **Goodwill**

Goodwill represents the value of all favorable attributes that relate to a company that is not tied to any other specific assets. These attributes include exceptional management, desirable location, good customer relations, skilled employees, highquality products, and harmonious relations with labor unions. Goodwill is unique. Unlike assets such as investments and plant assets, which can be sold individually in the marketplace, goodwill can be identified only with the business as a whole. There are two kinds of goodwill.

(1) Generated goodwill. **Generated goodwill** is something such as good reputation, which increases the value of the business. Generated goodwill cannot be quantified, so it doesn't belong to the category of accounting.

(2) Consolidated goodwill. Goodwill researched in accounting science is called consolidated goodwill. **Consolidated goodwill** is defined as the excess of the cost of purchasing another company over the sum of the market value of the acquired company's equity. A purchaser is willing to pay for goodwill when the purchaser buys another company

Plant Assets, Natural Resources, and Intangible Assets

which is believed to have strong profitability.

Goodwill is only recorded when the acquisition of another company happens. A purchase transaction provides objective evidence of the value of goodwill. Companies never record goodwill that they create for their own business. Goodwill is not amortized because it is considered to have an indefinite life. However, goodwill must be written down if a company determines that its value has been permanently impaired.

AAA Company's financial position is shown in EXHIBIT 6-6. On January 1, 2023, Blue Fly Corporation acquired AAA Company, and paid $120,000 cash.

EXHIBIT 6-6   AAA Company's Financial Position

December 31, 2022			
Assets($)		Liabilities($)	
Cash	8,000	Accounts payable	80,000
Supplies	82,000	Long-term debts	15,000
Equipment	52,000	Total liabilities	95,000
Building	40,000		
Total assets	182,000		

Total equity = Total assets − Total liabilities

Total equity = $182,000 − $95,000 = $87,000

The journal entry for this transaction is:

Dr: Cash	8,000
Supplies	82,000
Equipment	52,000
Buildings	40,000
Goodwill	33,000
Cr: Accounts payable	80,000
Long-term debts	15,000
Cash	120,000

6.7.2 Amortization of the Intangible Assets

An intangible asset is recorded at its acquisition cost. The residual value of most intangibles is zero. There are two kinds of intangibles.

- **Intangibles with Finite Lives that Can Be Measured**

We record amortization for these intangibles. Amortization expense is the title of the expense associated with intangibles. Amortization works like depreciation and it is usually computed on a straight-line basis. Amortization can be credited directly to the asset account as below.

Suppose that Blue Fly Corporation bought a patent on January 1, 2022, and paid cash of $100,000. On December 31, 2022, the book value should be $95,000. The journal entry for this transaction is:

 Dr: Amortization expense   5,000
  Cr: Patent   5,000

- **Intangibles with Indefinite Lives**

We record no amortization for these intangibles. Instead, we check them annually for any loss in value, and record a loss when it occurs. Goodwill is the most typical intangible asset with an indefinite life.

6.7.3 Research and Development Costs

Research and development costs are expenditures that may lead to patents, copyrights, new processes, and new products. Many companies spend considerable sums of money on research and development (R&D).

Research and development costs present accounting problems as it is sometimes difficult to assign these costs to specific projects. Also, there are uncertainties in identifying the amount and timing of future benefits. Costs in the research phase are always expensed as incurred. Costs in the development phase are expensed until specific criteria are met, primarily when technological feasibility is achieved.

For example, assume that Blue Fly Corporation spent $1 million on research and $2 million on development of new products. Of the $2 million in development costs, $400,000 was incurred prior to technological feasibility and $1,600,000 was incurred after technological feasibility had been demonstrated. The company would record these costs as follows.

 Dr: Research and development expenses   1,400,000
   Development costs   1,600,000
  Cr: Cash   3,000,000

Plant Assets, Natural Resources, and Intangible Assets

Core Words

Long-lived assets	长期资产(非流动资产)
Tangible assets	有形资产
Intangible assets	无形资产
Plant assets/Fixed assets	固定资产
Land	土地
Buildings	建筑物
Constructed buildings	自建建筑
Purchased buildings	外购建筑
Machinery	机械
Equipment	设备
Capitalized expenditures	资本化支出
Immediate expenses	直接费用
Depreciation	折旧
Book value	账面价值
Historical cost	历史成本
Accumulated depreciation	累计折旧
Estimated useful life	估计使用寿命
Estimated residual value	估计残值
Straight-line depreciation method	直线法(年限平均法)
Double-declining-balance depreciation method	双倍余额递减法
Units-of-production depreciation method	工作量法
Revaluation of plant assets	固定资产重估值
Revaluation surplus	重估价盈余
Impairment loss	减值损失
Other comprehensive income	其他综合收益
Gain on disposal	处置收益
Loss on disposal	处置损失
Natural resources	自然资源
Biological assets	生物资产
Depletion	(资源)耗减
Patents	专利权

Copyrights	版权
Trademarks	商标权
Franchises	特许经营权
Goodwill	商誉
Generated goodwill	自创商誉
Consolidated goodwill	外购商誉
Amortization	摊销
Finite lives	有限使用寿命
Indefinite lives	无限使用寿命
Research and development costs	研究和发展费用

Extended Reading

1. 固定资产

固定资产是指企业为生产产品、提供劳务、出租或者经营管理而持有的、使用时间超过12个月的、价值达到一定标准的非货币性资产,包括房屋、建筑物、机器、机械、运输工具以及其他与生产经营活动有关的设备、器具、工具等。

可选用的折旧方法包括年限平均法、工作量法、双倍余额递减法和年数总和法等。固定资产的折旧方法一经确定,不得随意变更。固定资产应当按月计提折旧,并根据其用途计入相关资产的成本或者当期损益。

值得注意的是,当月增加的固定资产,当月不计提折旧,从下月起计提折旧;当月减少的固定资产,当月仍计提折旧,从下月起停止计提折旧。固定资产提足折旧后,不管能否继续使用,均不再提取折旧;提前报废的固定资产,也不再补提折旧。

2. 无形资产

无形资产是指企业拥有或控制的没有实物形态的可辨认非货币性资产,通常包括专利权、非专利技术、商标权、著作权、特许权、版权等。

需要注意的是,我国实行土地公有制,所以土地是以土地使用权的形式作为无形资产入账的,而大多数资本主义国家都将土地直接作为固定资产来入账。在本章中,考虑到会计英语实际应用的意义,将土地作为固定资产进行讲解。

3. 商誉

我国会计准则规定，商誉是企业合并成本大于合并取得被购买方各项可辨认资产、负债公允价值份额的差额，其存在无法与企业自身分离，不具有可辨认性，不属于无形资产准则所规范的无形资产。但本书所提及的"商誉"适用美国的无形资产准则，确认为无形资产核算。对于我国准则规定的商誉的含义，需要把握以下5点：

(1) 商誉是在企业合并时产生的。投资方合并被投资方取得股权，有两种情况：一是同一控制下的企业合并取得股权，如企业集团内的企业合并；二是非同一控制下的企业合并取得股权。先前的无形资产准则规定的"企业自创商誉不能加以确认"在这个新准则中更加明确。

(2) 商誉的确认仅限于"正商誉"，不包括"负商誉"。即"企业合并成本大于合并取得被购买方各项可辨认资产、负债公允价值份额的差额"作为商誉(正商誉)处理；如果企业合并成本小于合并取得被购买方各项可辨认资产、负债公允价值份额的差额——负商誉，则计入当期损益。

(3) 商誉的确认以"公允价值"为基础。

(4) 商誉与企业自身不可分离，不具有可辨认性。

(5) 商誉不属于"无形资产"规范的内容。商誉按《企业会计准则第20号——企业合并》和《企业会计准则第33号——合并财务报表》的规定进行处理。

商誉在会计实务中指的是"商誉"会计科目，属于资产类科目，该科目期末借方余额，反映了企业商誉的价值。

4. 减税降费助力企业科技创新

科技型中小企业技术含量高，创新能力强，是极具活力和潜力的创新主体，其研发支出所占比例较大。2022年3月，国家将科技型中小企业研发费用税前加计扣除比例由75%提高至100%[①]，进一步支持科技型中小企业科技创新，给企业带来的是"真金白银"。对科技型中小企业来说，"创新"的背后蕴藏的是对多极化竞争的应对及未来发展的无限潜能。在深入实施创新驱动发展战略的大背景下，近年来，各级地方税务局积极发挥职能作用，通过大数据识别并建立符合政策条件的企业名录，采取税企微信、短信提醒、专题讲座等定向宣传培训方式，向科技型中小企业宣传、解读最新研究费用加计扣除政策和办税操作指南；同时为应享未享的企业提供"一对一"个性化辅导，确保政策红利直达企业，助力中小企业创新发展。大力度的税费优惠政策让企业在创新的道

---

① 资料来源：《关于进一步提高科技型中小企业研发费用税前加计扣除比例的公告》(财政部 税务总局 科技部公告 2022 年第 16 号)。

路上"轻装上阵",而研发投入的增加也让企业发展有了后劲。

本章节中我们深入学习了无形资产的各种形式,在国家大力发展科技兴国、支持自主创新的利好背景下,我们当代大学生是祖国的希望,也是全面实现创新创业的主要动力。为全面建成小康社会,推进社会主义现代化,实现中华民族伟大复兴,大学生不仅需要具备较高的科学文化素养和技能水平,还需要创新技术和科研成果的不断注入,因此大学生的主动科技创新意识显得尤为重要。

Exercises

1. All of the tangible assets need to be depreciated, except (   ).
   A. Plant
   B. Land
   C. Building
   D. Equipment

2. Which of the following can be identified as capital ized expenditures of a car? (   )
   A. Overhaul of the car.
   B. Repair of the car paint.
   C. Change of the engine oil.
   D. Car wash.

3. Which is the necessary item to calculate depreciation? (   )
   A. Historical book value.
   B. Estimated useful life.
   C. Estimated residual value.
   D. All of the above.

4. A company bought a new machine at $80,000 on January 1, 2021. The estimated residual value of the machine is $2,000, and the estimated useful life of the machine is 5 years. The company uses the straight-line method to record depreciation. What is the amount of accumulated depreciation on December 31, 2022? (   )
   A. $15,600.
   B. $31,200.
   C. $16,000.
   D. $32,000.

5. AAA company applies revaluation accounting to a piece of equipment that is recorded on its books at $800,000, with $100,000 of accumulated depreciation (after depreciation for the year is recorded). It has determined that the asset is now worth $775,000. The entry to record the revaluation would include a (   ).
   A. credit to equipment of $25,000
   B. debit to equipment of $75,000
   C. credit to accumulated depreciation of $100,000
   D. debit to revaluation surplus of $75,000

Plant Assets, Natural Resources, and Intangible Assets — Chapter 6

6. AAA company has decided to sell one of its old manufacturing machines on June 30, 2022. The machine was purchased at $80,000 on January 1, 2018, and was depreciated on a straight-line basis for 10 years. Assume the machine had no residual value. If the machine was sold for $26,000, what was the amount of the gain or loss recorded at the time of the sale?(   )

    A. $18,000.   C. $22,000.

    B. $54,000.   D. $46,000.

7. XYZ Energy company expects to extract 20 million tons of coal from a mine that costs $12 million. If no residual value is expected and 2 million tons are mined in the first year, the entry to record depletion will include a (   ).

    A. debit to accumulated depletion of $2,000,000

    B. credit to depletion expense of $1,200,000

    C. debit to inventory of $1,200,000

    D. credit to accumulated depletion of $2,000,000

8. Which method is used for amortization of intangible assets? (   )

    A. Straight-line method.

    B. Units-of-production method.

    C. Double-declining-balance method.

    D. All of the above.

9. Which of the following is not an intangible asset? (   )

    A. A patent.   B. A copyright.

    C. Land.   D. A trademark.

10. Which of the following statements is false? (   )

    A. If an intangible asset has a definite life, it should be amortized.

    B. The amortization period of an intangible asset can exceed 20 years.

    C. Goodwill is recorded only when a business is purchased.

    D. Development costs are always expensed when incurred.

11. Suppose that AAA Company bought a machine at $85,000 on January 1, 2018. The estimated useful life of the machine is 5 years, and its estimated residual value is $5,000.

    Requirement 1

    Use straight-line depreciation method to calculate depreciation expense, accumulated depreciation, and book value each year, and finish the form below.

	Annual depreciation	Accumulated depreciation	Book value
Jan.1, 2018			
Dec.31, 2018			
Dec.31, 2019			
Dec.31, 2020			
Dec.31, 2021			
Dec.31, 2022			

Requirement 2

Use DDB depreciation method to calculate depreciation expense, accumulated depreciation, and book value each year, and finish the form below.

	DDB rate	Annual depreciation	Accumulated depreciation	Book value
Jan.1, 2018				
Dec.31, 2018				
Dec.31, 2019				
Dec.31, 2020				
Dec.31, 2021				
Dec.31, 2022				

12. AAA company sold a piece of equipment on August 31, 2022, for $20,000 cash. The equipment originally cost $60,000 and as of January 1, 2022, had accumulated depreciation of $38,000. Depreciation for the first 8 months of 2022 was $6,000. Prepare the journal entries to

(1) update depreciation to August 31, 2020.

(2) record the sale of the equipment.

13. In 2022, BBB company had the following transactions related to intangible assets.

Jan.1, 2022 Purchased patent (8-year life) at $560,000.

Jul.1, 2022 10-year franchise; expiration date Jul. 1, 2032; $440,000.

Sep.1, 2022 Research and development costs, $185,000.

Instructions:

Prepare the necessary entries to record these intangibles. All costs incurred were in cash. Make the adjusting entries as of December 31, 2022, recording any necessary amortization and reflecting all balances accurately as of that date. Assume all development costs were incurred prior to technological feasibility.

Chapter 7
Liabilities

Spotlight

What could you do if you had an idea for new products but ran short of money? Are all expenses spent by a business paid in the accounting period in which they are incurred? What if a business is short of funds but has limited access to bank loans? With these questions in mind, let's look at Neila's Company.

Neila's Company mainly deals in fashion items. Their products, from clothing to backpacks, are popular among young girls. In order to implement the expansion strategy, Neila's Company has opened 80 new stores nationwide these years. To raise fund, the company borrowed money from banks and issued corporate bonds. The management believes that remaining competitive requires continual growth. The borrowed money could increase the sales and earnings, which could bring more benefits to the management and shareholders.

At the same time, there are still short-term arrears such as credit purchases and payables in the daily business. In this chapter, we will learn how companies account for money they owned or borrowed.

The liabilities section of Neila's Company's balance sheet is shown in EXHIBIT 7-1.

EXHIBIT 7-1 Neila's Company's Balance Sheet as of Dec. 31, 2022 ($ in Millions)

	2022	2021
Current liabilities		
Accounts payable	1,300	1,200
Short-term debts	900	950
Accrued liabilities	980	1,100
Current maturities of long-term debts	230	140
Total current liabilities	3,410	3,390
Long-term debts		
Long-term notes payable	900	800
Long-term bonds payable	1,150	900
Deferred income taxes	760	750
Other liabilities	520	450
Total long-term liabilities	3,330	2,900
Total debts	6,740	6,290

Text

Liabilities, which relate to the past transactions or events of an enterprise, are expected to be obligations to pay cash or to provide goods and services to other companies or individuals. Liabilities include wages due to employees, payables to suppliers, taxes owed, interest and principal due to lenders, obligations from losing a lawsuit, and so on. A liability arises whenever an organization recognizes an obligation before paying it. As our accounting process is based on the accrual basis, such liabilities are recognized as they occur, not necessarily when companies pay them in cash.

Liabilities can be classified into **current liabilities** and **long-term liabilities**, and such classification could help the financial statement analysis recognize the immediacy of the company's obligations. A current liability is a debt that a company expects to pay within one year or within the company's normal operating cycle (if that cycle is longer than one year). Debts that do not meet this criterion are non-current liabilities. The current liabilities include wages due to employees, payables to suppliers, taxes owed, and so on. The long-term liabilities include interest and principal due to lenders, such as the banks or the creditors. Companies usually pay long-term obligations gradually, yearly or monthly. Some obligations are paid in one large sum at maturity.

In the general ledger, companies keep separate accounts for different liabilities, such as wages, salaries, commissions, interest, and so on. In the annual report, however, companies often combine these liabilities and show them as a single account labeled "accrued liabilities" or "accrued expenses payable" as shown in EXHIBIT 7-1.

7.1 Accounting for Current Liabilities

7.1.1 Accounts Payable

Amounts owed for products or services purchased on account are **accounts payable.** One of a merchandising company's most common transactions is the credit purchase of inventory. For example, Neila's Company buys fabrics from other clothing manufacturers on account. Accounts payable is always set as a separate line item under current liabilities on the balance sheet.

Suppose that Neila's Company purchased a number of fabrics of $100,000 and appointed to make payments the next month. The journal entry for this transaction is shown as below:

    Dr: Inventory   100,000
        Cr: Accounts payable   100,000

7.1.2 Short-Term Notes Payable

Taking loans is a common form of financing. When companies take out loans, they need to sign promissory notes, which are shown on financial statements as **notes payable**. A promissory note is a written promise to repay the principal and interest on a specific date. Most promissory notes are payable to banks.

Notes are issued for varying periods of time. Those due for payment within one year of the balance sheet date are usually classified as current liabilities. If the obligation to repay the loan principal and interest is over one year, such obligation belongs to the long-term liabilities.

To illustrate the accounting for short-term notes payable, assume that Neila's Company took a 6-month-loan from the bank for $1,000,000 on March 1, 2022. The annual interest rate is 9%. The loan contract stipulates that the principal and interest should be paid in one lump sum at maturity.

The entry is as follows:

<u>March 1, 2022</u>
    Dr: Cash   1,000,000
        Cr: Notes payable   1,000,000

<u>March 31, 2022/April 30, 2022</u>
    Dr: Interest expense   7,500
        Cr: Interest payable   7,500
($1,000,000×9%×1/12=$7,500)

<u>May 31, 2022</u>
    Dr: Interest expense   7,500
        Interest payable   15,000
        Notes payable   1,000,000
        Cr: Cash   1,022,500

7.1.3 Sales Taxes Payable

Sales tax is neither revenue nor expense to a company. The company is simply serving as a collection agency for the taxing authority. When a retailer collects sales taxes from customers, a current liability is created until the company pays it to the government.

For example, if a customer pays a 6% sales tax on sales of $10,000, the total amount collected by Neila's Company will be $10,600 ($10,000 + $600).

The company can record the transaction as follows:

Sales day
   Dr: Cash   10,600
      Cr: Sales revenue   10,000
         Sales taxes payable   600

Tax payment day
   Dr: Sales taxes payable   600
      Cr: Cash   600

7.1.4 Value-added Taxes Payable

Value-added taxes (VAT) are levied in many countries around the world. In a VAT system, as the merchandise moves from the manufacturer to the wholesaler, to the retailer, and the consumer, a VAT is incurred at each point whenever value is added. Finally, a VAT is a cost to the end user, normally a private individual. A VAT should not be confused with a sales tax, because a sales tax is collected only once at the consumer's point of purchase.

To illustrate, assume that Neila's Company sold a batch of shoes to customers for $2,000, and the VAT was 10%. Neila's Company made the following entry to record the sale.

   Dr: Cash   2,200
      Cr: Sales revenue   2,000
         Value-added taxes payable   200

7.1.5 Accrued Liabilities

An accrued liability usually results from an expense that a company has incurred but not yet paid. The accrued expenses create liabilities. Hence, such expenses are also called accrued expenses. There are several kinds of accrued liabilities, such as salaries and wages payable and interest payable.

Employee compensation is the major expense for most service companies. There are several types of employee compensation. Annual or monthly payments are called *salaries*. A *wage* is a pay stated at an hourly rate. A salesperson usually gets *commission* according to his or her sales performance. As the payment of wages, salaries, and commissions happens frequently for most companies, such obligations are usually shown on the financial statements as a separate line, called **(accrued) wages payable, (accrued) salaries payable or (accrued) commissions payable.** Accounting for employee compensation is a complicated job, because employers must withhold some employee earnings and pay them instead to the government, insurance companies, social security department, and so on. The withholdings are not additional costs for the company. They are part of the employee wages and salaries that the company pays to third parties on behalf of the employees.

Suppose that Neila's Company has $100,000 of employee compensation. The income tax rate is 12%, and the FICA tax rate is 8%. The journal entry is as follows:

   Dr: Salaries and wages expense   100,000
       Cr: Employee income tax payable   12,000
           FICA tax payable   8,000
           Salaries and wages payable   80,000

7.1.6 Income Taxes Payable

In nearly every country in the world, companies have obligations to pay taxes to the government to keep the whole society running well. A typical one of them is **income taxes.** An income tax is a government levy imposed on individuals or entities that varies with the taxable income of the taxpayer. Corporations usually make periodic installment payments based on their estimated tax for the year instead of paying one lump sum at tax time. If the actual tax exceeds the estimated amount at the end of the year, the tax payable (or refund) occurs.

To illustrate, suppose Neila's Company had an estimated pre-tax income of $100,000 for the year 2021. At a 40% tax rate, the company's estimated income taxes for the year were $40,000. The company was expected to pay the income taxes as shown in EXHIBIT 7-2 (assume the company has equal quarterly payments).

EXHIBIT 7-2 Neila's Company's Estimated Income Taxes

	April 15	June 15	September 15	December 15
Estimated taxes	$10,000	$10,000	$10,000	$10,000

As we know, in most cases, the estimated pre-tax income could not be the same as the final exact income at the end of the year. Therefore, Neila's Company must file a final income tax return and make a final payment on March 15, 2022. Suppose the actual pre-tax income for the year 2021 was $105,000 instead of the estimated $100,000. Total tax would then be $42,000. By the payment date of the next year, the company must pay the additional income tax of $2,000.

The journal entry for the extra income tax payable is:

 Dr: Income taxes expense   2,000
  Cr: Income taxes payable   2,000

The journal entry for the payment date is:

 Dr: Income taxes payable   2,000
  Cr: Cash   2,000

7.1.7 Unearned Revenue

Unearned revenue is also called **deferred revenue** or **revenue collected in advance.** Some companies usually collect cash from customers before they deliver services or goods, such as airlines, magazine publishers, theatres, and so on. These unearned revenues are current liabilities for the reason that companies have obligations either to deliver the products or to provide services for the customers.

When a company receives an advance payment, it debits cash and credits the unearned revenue. After providing goods or services for the customers, the company can then recognizes the revenue.

Let's consider an example: on May 31, 2022, Butterfly Theatre sold 5,000 season tickets at $80 each for a series of four performances.

The theatre made the following entry for the sale of season tickets.

On May 31, 2022

 Dr: Cash   400,000
  Cr: Unearned ticket revenue   400,000

When all the shows were completed, Butterfly Theatre recognized the revenue with the following entry.

On June 10, 2022

 Dr: Unearned ticket revenue   400,000
  Cr: Ticket revenue   400,000

7.1.8 Current Portion of Long-term Debts

Some long-term debts could be paid in installments, so companies often have a portion of long-term debts that comes due in the current year. This part is considered as a current liability. The **current portion of long-term debts** (also called **current maturity or current installment**), which is the amount of the principal that is payable within one year, should be reclassified from the long-term liability to a current liability.

For example, assume that Neila's Company issued a five-year note for $50,000 on January 1, 2020. This note specifies that Neila's Company should pay $10,000 of the note on each January 1, starting from January 1, 2021. When the company prepared financial statements on December 31, 2020, it should report $10,000 as a current liability and $40,000 as a non-current liability.

On December 31, 2020

Dr: Long-term debts   10,000

    Cr: Current maturities of long-term debts   10,000

7.2　Liabilities with Uncertainty

Sometimes a business has some uncertain liabilities. For example, if a company is involved in a lawsuit that might result in financial loss or even bankruptcy in the future, how should the company deal with this major contingency? Sometimes the company needs to make a **provision** for liabilities with uncertainty. A provision is a liability of uncertain timing or amount. However, once the event happens, it will have an impact on the financial situation of the entity, so the company needs to make a disclosure. Common types of provisions are obligations related to litigation expense, **warranty expense**, product guarantees, and so on.

Companies can identify an expense and related liabilities for a provision when the following three conditions are met:

(1) It is a present obligation resulting from past events.

(2) The occurrence of the event will "probably" lead to the outflow of economic interests of the entity.

(3) The outflow of economic benefits can be reliably estimated.

It's worth noting that "probably" in condition (2) is defined as "more likely than not to occur". Usually the probability of occurrence is greater than 50%. If the probability is 50% or less, the provision will not be recognized.

Product warranty is a common estimated liability. It is a promise to repair or replace a defective product, usually for problems that arise within a specified period of time or usage. The accounting for warranty costs is based on the expense recognition principle. The estimated cost of honoring product warranty contracts should be recognized as an expense in the period in which the sale occurs.

For example, Brown Company is a dishwasher manufacturer. It made a total sale of $100,000 this year. The company provides product warranty for every dishwasher machine sold for 2 years. This means that within the warranty period, if there is a quality problem, the company is responsible for repair. Judging from previous experience, maintenance is 4% of sales. In this case, Brown Company could estimate a warranty expense of $4,000 ($100,000×4%) for the year and make the following entry:

    Dr: Warranty expense   4,000
        Cr: Estimated warranty payable   4,000

7.3 Accounting for Long-term Liabilities

Long-term liabilities are obligations that would be due over one year. Long-term liabilities conclude two main items: bonds and notes payable. Large companies can borrow millions of dollars from banks for several years by signing promissory notes, which become **long-term notes payable** on the balance sheet. But they cannot borrow billions of dollars from a single lender, so how do corporations collect huge sums? They issue **bonds** to the public which become **bonds payable.** How exactly do lenders and borrowers measure the value of such long-term obligations? They use the time value of money, which means that a dollar you expect to pay or receive in the future may not be worth as much as a dollar you have today.

7.3.1 Bonds: an Introduction

Large corporations have heavy demands for borrowed capital, so they often issue corporation **bonds** to the public in the financial markets. The purchaser of a bond receives the bond's formal certificate, which carries the **principal, the payment date,** and **interest rate.** The principal is also called the bond's face value, maturity value, or par value. The certificate also states the issuing company should pay the debt at a specific future time called the **maturity date**.

We regard the interest as the rental fee on borrowed money of the issuing company. The issuing company should pay the interest at a specified annual rate at a fixed **interest rate** on the bond's certificate. The interest rate is also called the **nominal interest rate, contractual rate, coupon rate,** or **stated rate.** The issuing company generally pays interest for the bonds every month or every 6 months.

7.3.2 Types of Bonds

- **Mortgage Bonds and Subordinated Debentures**

When a company is in liquidation, the bond provisions determine the bondholders' priority for their claims and the amount the bondholders could get from the liquidating assets and cash. The **mortgage bonds** and **subordinated debentures** have different priorities for the claims.

The **mortgage bonds** are secured by the agreed specific property in the covenants, which means these bondholders have the first right to the claims of the specific property in the liquidating process.

In contrast, the **subordinated debenture** holders are not secured by any property in their bond covenants, which means they have a lower priority to collect their amount of bond.

- **Callable and Convertible Bonds**

A **callable bond**, or **redeemable bond**, gives the bond issuer the right to purchase the bond back from the bond holder before the maturity date of the bond through an embedded call option. The issuer will compensate the bond holder with an option premium to purchase the bond back.

In finance, a **convertible bond** is a type of bond that can be converted into a specified number of shares of common stock in the issuing company or cash of equal value. Because of the conversion superiority, convertible bonds usually have a lower interest rate than similar bonds without the conversion privilege.

7.3.3 Issuing Bonds

There are three ways for corporations to issue bonds: **issuing at par, issuing at premium, and issuing at discount.** The issuing types are determined by the **market rate and the coupon rate.** The market rate is the rate available to invest in similar bonds at a moment in time. It is the interestrate that investors require if they are tending to purchase the bond. A bond issued at a price which is equal to its face value is called a bond **issued at par.** In some situations, the bond's market rate differs from the coupon rate. A bond issued at a price higher than its face value is called a bond **issued at premium**, and in contrast, a bond issued at a price below its face value is called a bond **issued at discount.**

Issuing Bonds Payable at Par

Suppose that on January 1, 2022, Neila's Company issued 1 billion, 2-year, annual 10% interest debentures, at par, which means the market rate is equal to the coupon rate and there is no premium or discount on these bonds payable.

The company has to pay back the principal of $ 1 billion two years later and the company must pay the interest for such bonds every half year. The interest expense equals the amount of the interest payment: 10% × $1 billion × 1/2 = $50 million every 6 months for a total of $200 million over the four semiannual periods. EXHIBIT 7-3 shows how the bonds affect Neila's Company's balance sheet equation in its 2-year life (assume the company does not retire them before maturity).

EXHIBIT 7-3 Bond Transactions: Issued at Par ($ in Millions)

	Assets	=	Liabilities	+	Stockholders' Equity
	Cash		Bonds payable		Retained earnings
Issuer's records					
(1) Issuance	+1,000	=	+1,000		
(2)-(5) Semiannual interest (repeated twice a year for 2 years)	−50	=			Increase interest expense −50
(6) Maturity value (final payment)	−1,000	=	−1,000		

The journal entries are:

(1) Dr: Cash	1,000,000,000	
Cr: Bonds payable		1,000,000,000
(2)-(5) Dr: Interest expense	50,000,000	
Cr: Cash		50,000,000
(6) Dr: Bonds payable	1,000,000,000	
Cr: Cash		1,000,000,000

Entry (1) is at issuance, entries (2) through (5) are the four identical interest payments, and entry (6) is the repayment of principal at maturity.

Issuing Bonds Payable at a Discount

On January 1, 2022, Neila's Company issued 1 billion, 2-year, annual 10% interest debentures. The annual market interest rate is 12%, which means the rate for each six-month period is 6%. We can recognize that the market rate is higher than the coupon rate, which means that the issuer has to decrease the issuing price, or no investor would choose such a bond with a lower interest rate. However, how can we determine the amount of discount? By checking the present value table, we get the present value factor as shown in EXHIBIT 7-4.

EXHIBIT 7-4

Computation of Market Value of $1 Billion Principal, 10% Coupon, 2-year Bond ($in Millions)

	Present value factor	Total present value
Valuation at market rate of 12% per year, or 6% per half-year		
Principal	0.792,1	792.10
Interest	3.465,1	173.25
Total		965.35

Neila's Company could only collect $965.35 million for issuing such bonds. Therefore, the company recognized a discount of $1,000 − $965.35 = $34.65 million at issuance. The journal entry at issuance should be:

  Dr: Cash   965,350,000

    Discount on bonds payable   34,650,000

    Cr: Bonds payable   1,000,000,000

When making the bookkeeping of this discount on bonds payable, please note that the discount is a contra account. The bonds payable account on the books usually shows the face value, deducting the discount amount from the face amount, and then we get the amount shown in the balance sheet(see EXHIBIT 7-5), which is often referred to as the net liability.

EXHIBIT 7-5 Issuer's Balance Sheet

Issuer's Balance Sheet	Jan. 1, 2022
Bonds payable, 10% due Dec. 31, 2023	$1,000,000,000
Deduct: Discount on bonds payable	$34,650,000
Net liability (book value)	$965,350,000

- **Bonds Issued at a Premium**

Again, we suppose that on January 1, 2022, Neila's Company issued 1 billion, 2-year, annual 10% interest debentures. The annual market interest rate is 8%, which means the rate for each six-month period is 4%. In this example, the coupon rate exceeds the market rate, which could lead to a loss of the issuer because the issuer gives a higher interest rate than others in the same market. We still use the present value table to check out the present value factor on 4% with four periods as shown in EXHIBIT 7-6.

EXHIBIT 7-6 Computation of Market Value of $1 Billion Principal, 10% Coupon, 2-year Bond ($ in Millions)

	Present value factor	Total present value
Valuation at market rate of 8% per year, or 4% per half-year		
Principal	0.8548	854.80
Interest	3.6299	181.50
Total		1,036.30

As Neila's Company issued a higher coupon rate, the bonds were issued at a premium to cover the interest loss. The company could receive $1,036.3 million for the bonds. Balance sheets show the net liability calculated as the face amount plus the unamortized premium.

    Dr: Cash   1,036,300,000
        Cr: Premium on bonds payable   36,300,000
            Bonds payable   1,000,000,000

Core Words

Liabilities	负债
Current liability	流动负债
Long-term liability	长期负债
Accounts payable	应付账款
Notes payable	应付票据
Sales taxes payable	应交销售税
Value-added taxes payable	应交增值税
Accrued liabilities	应计负债
Accrued expenses	应计费用
Accrued employee compensation	应付职工薪酬
Income taxes payable	应交所得税
Current portion of long-term debts	1年内到期长期负债
Unearned revenue	预收账款
Provision	准备金

Warranty expense	保修费用
Debenture	债券
Corporate bonds	公司债券
Stated rate	票面利率
Par value	面值
Mortgage bond	抵押债券
Subordinated debenture	次级债券
Callable bonds	可赎回债券
Convertible bonds	可转换债券
Market rate	市场利率
Bond discount	债券折价
Bond premium	债券溢价

Extended Reading

1. 流动负债的中外比较

1) 有关流动负债的概念在外延及内涵上不尽相同

美国财务会计准则委员会在1980年的第3号财务概念公告中，将流动负债定义为："将在一年或一个正常的经营周期内，并期望要求应用那些已经适当地划分为流动资产的现有来源，或通过产生其他流动负债来加以清偿的责任。"而我国《企业会计准则》将流动负债定义为："将在一年内或超过一年的一个营业周期内偿还的债务。"

从两者所下的定义可看出，西方关于流动负债概念的规定有两个特点：一是在内容上，将流动资产与流动负债联系起来，考虑了它们之间的相互联系，从而有助于正确地反映企业的财务状况；二是在时间上，不机械地以"一年"为界，这样就考虑了不同企业的不同经营周期，从而能客观地反映流动负债的"流动"特征。我国新制度对流动负债下的定义同样不机械地以"一年"为界，但未将流动资产与流动负债联系起来。

2) 有关流动负债的财务处理及界定方法不一致

从我国颁布的有关财务制度中不难看出，其所指的负债都是现实的负债。而西方国家在会计处理上则不同，其所指的负债不仅指现实的负债，还包括未来可能发生的负债——或有负债。

2. 可转换债券的中外会计处理差异

所谓可转换债券，是指持有者可以在一定时期内按一定比例或价格将信用债券转换成一定数量的普通股票的债券。可转换债券既不同于传统股票，也不同于传统债券，而是一种兼债权与股权性质于一身的混合式金融工具。一方面，它具有明显的债券性质，如果投资者在转换期内未将其转换为股票，发行人必须无条件地还本付息；另一方面，可转换债券又具有股权性质，持有人可在规定的时间内按条件将其转换为普通股，在转换之后，由被投资企业的债务转为股本。在规定的转换期内，投资者既可以选择行使转换权，也可以放弃转换权利。这种混合性对现存的会计实务提出了挑战：到底是把可转换债券作为债务处理，还是作为权益处理？

1) 国内的处理方法

2006年，我国财政部颁发新会计准则及指南，对可转换债券等金融衍生工具的会计处理做出了以下规定。

对于发行方，企业发行的某些非衍生金融工具(如可转换公司债券等)既含有负债成分，又含有权益成分，应在初始确认时，将相关负债和权益成分进行拆分，先对负债成分的未来现金流量进行折现，确定负债成分的初始金额，再按发行收入扣除负债成分的差额，确认权益成分的初始金额。对于发行费用，应当在负债成分和权益成分之间按其初始确认金额的相对比例进行分摊。

对于投资方，同样要求对取得的可转换债券的负债部分和权益部分分别进行确认。对负债部分，应按债券的面值，借记可供出售金融资产(成本)，按实际支付的金额，贷记"银行存款"等科目，按差额，借记或贷记"可供出售金融资产(利息调整)"。

2) 国外的处理方法

ED59(国际会计准则59号草案)对可转换债券的处理方法跟我国方法存在很大不同。根据ED59的规定，在发行时也是采用折现的方法，确定权益部分价值，但是发行后的处理则是运用实际利率法将"应付债券"调整为债券面值，如债券到期没有实现转换，则要确认留存收益；如实现转换，则将权益部分价值连同债券账面价值一并进行转股处理。

3. "税"的力量

税收是指国家为了向社会提供公共产品，满足社会共同需要，参与社会产品的分配，按照法律的规定，强制、无偿取得财政收入的一种规范形式。税收具有强制性、无偿性、固定性，是经济运行的重要手段和有力杠杆，亦是一种非常重要的政策工具。

税收的力量很大，能推动国家、社会发展；税收的力量也很温柔，虽然我们看不到它，但它跟我们每一个人的生活都息息相关。

因此无论是企业还是个人，都应该按照税法的规定按时缴纳税金，尽到每个公民应尽的义务。

Exercises

1. Which of the following is not a current liability? (   )

    A. Accounts payable.

    B. Wages payable.

    C. Current-portion of long-term debts.

    D. Bonds payable.

2. A contingent liability should be recorded in the accounts (   ).

    A. if the amount can be vaguely estimated

    B. if the amount is due in cash within one year

    C. if the related future event will probably occur

    D. none of the above

3. The discount on a bond payable is (   ).

    A. a reduction in interest expense

    B. an expense at the bond's maturity

    C. a contra account to bonds payable

    D. an expense account

4. Issuing bonds is a/an (   ).

    A. operating activity   B. financing activity

    C. investing activity   D. payment activity

5. Suppose a company took out a loan from a local bank for $1,000,000. This loan would be paid during the next 5 years. The correct journal entry for this transaction is (   ).

    A. debit account receivable   B. debit note receivable

    C. credit note payable   D. credit cash

6. Which of the following bonds has the highest interest rate? (   )

    A. Callable bond.   B. Mortgage bond.

    C. Convertible bond.   D. Normal debentures.

7. When the coupon rate is over the market rate, which of the following is not correct? (   )

   A. The bond should be issued at a premium.

   B. The bond should be issued at a discount.

   C. The issuer can receive more cash than the bonds' face value.

   D. None of the above.

8. Which of the following is not a liability? (   )

   A. Unearned revenue.

   B. Deferred income taxes.

   C. Prepaid rent.

   D. Long-term note payable.

9. Which of the following illustrations is correct? (   )

   A. The mortgage bonds are secured by the agreed specific property.

   B. A convertible bond is a type of bond that can be converted into a specified number of shares of common stock in the issuing company or cash of equal value.

   C. A callable bond gives the bond issuer the right to purchase the bond back from the bond holder before the maturity date of the bond through an embedded call option.

   D. All the above.

10. When the bond's issuer collected less cash than the bond's face value, it means that (   ).

    A. the bond is issued at a premium

    B. the coupon rate is higher than the market rate

    C. the bond has to be issued at a discount

    D. the market interest rate is not stable

11. Name and briefly describe several items that are often classified as current liabilities.

12. "The face amount of a bond is what you can sell it for." Do you agree? Explain.

13. On February 25, Caleny Company paid the employee compensation for a total $10,000 and still owed $2,000 to be paid on March 25.

(1) Prepare the journal entry for recording the compensation expense for February.

(2) Suppose the total compensation expense for March is $15,000 and this would be paid on March 25 in total. How much cash would Caleny Company pay on March 25? Prepare the journal entry.

14. Steven Ltd. is a shoe company. It realized a total $5,000,000 pre-tax earning for the whole year of 2022. The company had paid income taxes (estimated) of 2022 of $1,800,000 monthly. If the income tax rate is 40%, calculate how much income tax the company has not paid yet, and prepare the journal entries.

15. The Union Inc., one of the largest airline companies in the world, had unearned revenues of $450 million on May 30, 2022. Suppose that during June, the Union Inc. had a realized sales revenue of 3 parts: $300 for prepaid customers, $200 for customers taking the airline in June, and $320 for customers that would take plane in the next month or later.

(1) Prepare the journal entry for the unearned revenues on May 30.
(2) Prepare the journal entries for the realized sales revenue during June.

16. Pepper Co., which is a chain restaurant, had the following items on its balance sheet of December 31, 2022 ($ in thousands):

Cash and cash equivalents	32,000
Accounts payable	14,500
Deferred income taxes	10,000
Retained earnings	108,900
Accrued expenses	20,100
Prepaid expenses	3,580
Short-term debts	11,580
Current maturities of long-term debts	3,830
Arbitration award	9,880
Long-term debts	50,300
Other long-term liabilities	5,216

Prepare the liabilities section of Pepper Corporation's balance sheet. Include only the items that are properly included in liabilities. Separate current and long-term liabilities.

Chapter 8
Stockholders' Equity

Spotlight

In your daily life, do you prefer to take a gasoline car or an electric car? We have many brand choices when deciding to buy a car. HH company, as one of the industry's top electric vehicle enterprises in all regions of the world, has been widely concerned and welcomed. The company started in 2003 and first offered the company's stock to the public in 2010. Now HH company has 6 factories and over 100,000 employees across the world.

During 2022, HH company reported sales of $10 million and a net income of $5 million. As the company had realized net earnings for 10 consecutive years, at the end of year 2022, the company made dividends of $1 million to its stockholders. EXHIBIT 8-1 shows the balance sheet of HH company.

So far, we've focused on deals that affect assets and liabilities, and now let's have a closer look at shareholders' equity. At the same time, other elements relating to owners' equity are also presented—additional paid-in capital, retained earnings, treasury stock, and dividends. After all, shareholders want to know the details of their investments. In addition, shareholders provide most of the capital needed to run a company, so understanding the rights and responsibilities of shareholders is important.

The accounting equation must be balanced. If we know the amount of assets and liabilities, shareholders' equity is the surplus, the difference between assets and liabilities. Therefore, we refer to shareholders as the residual claimants of the company. When a company fails and sells its assets to pay off creditors, shareholders get the rest of the value.

EXHIBIT 8-1 The Consolidated Balance Sheet of HH Corporation

HH Corp. Consolidated Balance Sheet December 31, 2022 ($ in thousands, except number of shares)	
Assets	
Current assets:	
Total current assets	25,300
Long-term receivables	10,000

Stockholders' Equity — Chapter 8

(Continued)

HH Corp. Consolidated Balance Sheet December 31, 2022 ($ in thousands, except number of shares)	
Property and equipment, net	32,000
Other assets	22,500
Total assets	89,800
Liabilities and Stockholders' Equity	
Current liabilities	
Total current liabilities	30,500
Long-term debts	10,500
Other long-term liabilities	4,800
Total liabilities	45,800
Stockholders' Equity	
Preferred stock, $2 par value, 10,000,000 shares authorized; shares issued and outstanding: none	—
Common stock, $1 par value, 6,000,000 shares authorized; 5,000,000 shares issued and 4,000,000 shares outstanding	4,000
Additional paid-in capital	11,000
Retained earnings	30,000
Treasury stock, at cost (1,000,000 shares)	(1,000)
Total stockholders' equity	44,000
Total liabilities and stockholders' equity	768,870

Text

8.1 Background and Definition of Owners' Equity

According to IFRS, a corporation is a permanently valid business entity established under state law. A corporation is an independent entity controlled by the stockholders or shareholders. The shareholders usually have many rights, for example:

(1) Vote. The shareholders have voting rights; they can participate in major corporate decisions.

(2) Dividends. The shareholders have the right to receive dividends from the net income of the company.

(3) Liquidation. Once a company is in liquidation, the shareholders can share the remaining assets after other creditors.

(4) Preemption. It refers to the right of the shareholders to preferentially purchase other shareholders' shares to be transferred under the same conditions.

Owners' equity refers to the residual equity enjoyed by the owners after deducting liabilities from the assets of the enterprise.

Shareholders' equity is divided into 3 main parts:

(1) Paid-in capital. This is a shareholder's contribution to the company, which is one part of the shareholders' equity. Paid-in capital includes stock accounts and any additional paid-in capital.

(2) Retained earnings. This is a big part of shareholders' equity, which is the amount the company has earned through profitable operations and has not used for dividends.

The owners' equity of a corporation is divided into shares of **stock**. Because stock represents the corporation's capital, it can also be called **capital stock**. As shown in EXHIBIT 8-1, the company issued 5,000,000 shares with $1 par value to the market. A corporation issues stock certificates to its owners when the company receives investment. The shareholders could apply dividends by their stock certificates. The basic unit of capital stock is 1 share. A corporation may issue a stock certificate for any number of shares—34,620 or any other number, but the total number of authorized shares is limited by charter.

To understand the shares of issued stock, we need to understand the relationship among different forms of shares: the authorized shares, issued shares, outstanding shares, and treasury stock.

Authorized stock is the maximum number of shares that a company can legally issue under the articles of incorporation. Through EXHIBIT 8-1, we see HH is authorized to issue 10,000,000 shares of stock.

Issued stock refers to the number of shares issued by a company to its shareholders. This is a cumulative total from the beginning of the company to the current date. As of December 31, 2022, HH had issued 5,000,000 shares of its common stock.

Treasury stock. This kind of stock is sold by its issuer and later bought back by the issuer. Note that the owner of such a stock has no voting rights.

Outstanding stock refers to the number of shares in a listed company owned by the shareholders, which is the number of shares in circulation in the hands of the shareholders. On December 31, 2022, HH had 4,000,000 shares of common stock outstanding, which were computed as follows:

Issued shares	5,000,000
Less: Treasury shares	1,000,000
Outstanding shares	4,000,000

According to IFRS, the number of authorized shares is set by the government and national laws, and a corporation is not allowed to issue shares without a limit. When a corporation issues shares to investors and receives cash, the shares become **issued stock**. But sometimes corporations buy back shares from their shareholders. The stock held by the corporation is called **treasury stock**. We will discuss treasury stock later in this section. When we subtract the shares of treasury stock from the number of issued stock, we get the remaining shares known as outstanding stock that remain in the hands of the shareholders other than the company itself.

(3) Other comprehensive income. It refers to the profits and losses that are not recognized in the current profits and losses according to other accounting standards.

8.2 The Classification of Stocks

8.2.1 Common Stock

Common stock is the basic form of company shares. The rights of common stockholders (or shareholders) generally include the right to (1) vote, (2) share in corporate profits through the declaration of dividends and/or appreciation of the share price, (3) share in any assets left at liquidation, and (4) possibly acquire shares of subsequent issues of stock. The extent of an individual stock-holder's power is determined by the number and type of shares held by the stockholder.

8.2.2 Preferred Stock

Preferred stock offers the stockholder different rights and preferential treatment over common stockholders. The terms of preferred stock can include almost any arrangement the company and stockholders agree upon.

Each of the following features can also affect the attractiveness of preferred stock. For example, a holder of participating preferred stock ordinarily receives a fixed dividend but can receive higher dividends when the company has a very good year—one in which common stockholders receive especially large dividends. **"Participating"** means that holders of these preferred shares participate in the growth of the company because they can share in growing dividends. If preferred stock does not have the participation feature, the dividend received by the preferred stockholder will be capped at the prespecified rate. If preferred stock is **callable**, the issuing company will have the right to purchase the stock back from the owner at specified dates upon payment of the **call price**, or **redemption price**. This call price is typically set above the par value or issuance price of the stock to compensate investors for the fact that the stock can be bought back at the issuer's choice. Recall from Chapter 7 that bonds may also be callable.

Convertible preferred stock gives the owner the option to exchange the preferred share for a prespecified number of shares of common stock. Because the ability to convert the stock can be quite valuable in future years if common stock prices grow significantly, convertible securities typically carry a lower dividend rate.

Preferred stock is a mixture of common stock and bond. Like bond, preferred stock pays a fixed dividend, which is similar to bond interest. But, like stock, the dividend does not have to be paid unless the board of directors declares the dividend. EXHIBIT 8-2 shows the similarities and differences between preferred stock and bond.

EXHIBIT 8-2   The Similarities and Differences Between Preferred Stock and Bond

	Bond	**Preferred stock**
Similarities	Both pay a specific return to the investor	
Differences	Interest	Dividend
	Taxable to recipient Tax deductible to the issuing company	Not tax deductible to the issuer. Fully taxed, partly taxed, or untaxed to the recipient
	Reduce income before tax	Reduce net income and retained earnings directly
	Have specific maturity dates	Have unlimited life

8.3 Issuing Stock

Most corporations need to raise huge amounts of money to keep their operations going or to expand the corporation size. Issuing stock to the public is the most crucial form of financing. Corporations can sell shares either directly or through underwriters, such as banks.

8.3.1 Common Stock at Par

In EXHIBIT 8-1, HH's common stock carried a par value of $1 per share. If the company issued 500,000 shares at par to the market, the journal entry would be:

Dr: Cash 500,000
    Cr: Common stock 500,000

The effect of this transaction would increase HH's assets and stockholders' equity by the same amount as follows:

Assets	=	Liabilities	+	Stockholders' equity
+500,000	=	0	+	500,000

8.3.2 Common Stock Above Par

Most corporations choose to issue common stock at a low par value and at a price above par. The value of common stock is usually divided into two parts: the par value of common stock and the additional paid-in capital.

Suppose HH's common stock has a par value of $1 per share and the company issued the stock with a market price of $6 per share. The $5 difference between the issue price ($6) and par value ($1) is additional paid-in capital. With 500,000 shares issued by par value of $1, HH's actual entry with a market price of $6 per share to record the issuance of common stock is as follows:

Dr: Cash 3,000,000
    Cr: Common stock 500,000
        Additional paid-in capital 2,500,000

The effect of this transaction would increase HH's assets and stockholders' equity by the same amount as follows:

Assets	=	Liabilities	+	Stockholders' equity
+3,000,000	=	0	+	500,000 + 2,500,000

8.4 Cash Dividends

Dividends are proportional distributions of the income to shareholders, usually in the form of cash. However, a corporation must satisfy two conditions when distributing dividends:

(1) There are sufficient retained earnings to declare dividends.

(2) Have enough cash to pay cash dividends.

A company's board of directors votes to approve each dividend and the company would not automatically pay dividends regularly. Only when the board of directors has declared a dividend, could the corporation declare a dividend to the shareholders. Once declared, the dividend becomes a legal liability of the company, which becomes a **dividend payable** account.

There are three relevant dates for dividends distributed.

1. Declaration Date

Declaration date is the date when the board of directors formally announces that it will pay a cash dividend. On this date, the dividend becomes a liability.

Suppose that $100,000 of cash dividend is declared:

  Dr: Retained earnings   100,000
   Cr: Dividends payable   100,000

2. Date of Record

Date of record is the date that determines which shareholders will receive a cash dividend. All stockholders owning stock on that date will receive the dividend. A person who holds the stock on the declaration date but sells before the date of record will not receive the dividend.

3. Payment Date

The actual payment date is the day when the company distributes the cash; it usually follows the date of record by a few days or weeks. On this date the company mails the checks to the shareholders. But if a person holds the stock on the declaration date, but sells it before the date of record, he or she will not receive the dividend.

A company records entries for cash dividends in two situations: when it creates the liability and when it pays the dividend. The payment is recorded by debiting dividends payable and crediting cash.

  Dr: Dividends payable   100,000
   Cr: Cash   100,000

8.5 Stock Dividends

Stock dividends are also distributions of additional shares to existing shareholders without additional consideration provided by the stockholders. However, the relative number of new shares issued is usually smaller than that in a split, although this is not a requirement. More importantly, a stock dividend increases the number of shares but does not change the per share par value. Consequently, the total par value of common stock reported on the balance sheet increases.

For example, assume you own 100 shares of HH's stock and the corporation distributes a 10% stock dividend, which means the issuance of 1 new share for every 10 shares currently owned will bring you 10 (100*10%) additional shares. As a result, you will own 110 shares of HH's common stock. All other HH's shareholders will also receive 10% additional shares, leaving all common stockholders' proportionate ownership unchanged.

The reasons that corporations choose stock dividends instead of cash dividends might be:

(1) To **conserve cash.** Companies may wish to continue to distribute the dividends to stockholders whilst retaining as much cash as possible to keep operating or expanding the corporation. Therefore, the company may distribute a stock dividend. In addition, the stock dividend would not require stockholders to pay income taxes on such benefits.

(2) Reducing market price per share of common stock distribution of a stock dividend could increase the number of outstanding shares. With a fixed profit, the increasing share numbers could lead the common stock's market price to fall. The lower market price per share could attract more investors.

8.5.1 Large-percentage Stock Dividends

Large-percentage stock dividends occur when the number of new shares issued exceeds 20% to 25% of the shares outstanding prior to the distribution. Companies account for large-percentage stock dividends at par or stated value. This means that an accounting entry simply transfers the par or stated value of the new shares from the retained earnings or additional paid-in capital account to the common stock account. While the debt side of this entry can, in practice, be to either retained earnings or additional paid-in capital, for our purposes we will assume the debt is to retained earnings.

Suppose HH corporation declared and distributed a 30% stock dividend at par value $1 to the shareholders with total 400,000 outstanding shares. This transaction would debit retained earnings and credit common stock for the par value of the shares.

  Dr: Retained earnings   120,000
    Cr: Common stock   120,000

8.5.2 Small-percentage Stock Dividends

Companies account for stock dividends of less than 20% to 25% at market value, not at par value. This rule is partly resulting from the tradition and partly because of the fact that small-percentage stock dividends are more likely to accompany increases in the total dividend payments or other changes in the company's financial policies. Security analysts argue that the decision to increase total cash dividends communicates the management's conviction that future cash flows will rise to support these increased distributions. This is a positive statement about a firm's prospects.

Suppose that HH corporation declared and distributed a 20% stock dividend at par value $1 and market price of $5 to the shareholders with total 400,000 outstanding shares. This transaction would debit retained earnings and credit common stock for the par value of the shares.

Dr: Retained earnings	400,000
Cr: Common stock	80,000
Additional paid-in capital	320,000

8.5.3 Fractional Shares

Corporations ordinarily issue shares in whole units, but sometimes shareholders are entitled to stock dividends in amounts equal to fractional units. For instance, HH corporation distributes a 3% stock dividend with a market price of $5 and par value of $1 to the shareholders.

If one shareholder has 160 shares, the shareholder would be entitled to $160 \times 0.03 = 4.8$ shares. In such a situation, corporations issue additional shares for whole units plus cash equal to the market value of the fractional amount.

As a result, the company would issue 4 shares plus $0.8 \times \$5 = \$4$ cash. The journal entry is as below:

Dr: Retained earnings (4.8×$5)	24
Cr: Common stock, at par (4×$1)	4
Additional paid-in capital(4×$4)	16
Cash	4

Core Words

Stockholders' equity	所有者权益
Paid-in capital	实收资本
Retained earnings	留存收益

Capital stock	股本
Common stock	普通股
Preferred stock	优先股
Par value	面值
Authorized stock	额定股本
Issued stock	已发行股票
Outstanding stock	流通股
Treasury stock	库存股
Cash dividends	现金股利
Stock options	优先认股权
Vested options	股票期权
Stock split	股票分割
Stock dividends	股票股利
Large-percentage stock dividends	大比例股票股利
Small-percentage stock dividends	小比例股票股利
Liquidation	破产清算
Preemption	优先购买权
Declaration date	股利宣告日
Date of record	股权登记日
Payment date	股利支付日

Extended Reading

1. 留存收益

留存收益是公司在经营过程中所创造的，由于公司经营发展的需要或法定的原因等，没有分配给所有者而留存在公司的盈利。留存收益是指企业从历年实现的利润中提取或留存于企业的内部积累，它来源于企业的生产经营活动所实现的净利润，包括企业的盈余公积金和未分配利润两个部分，其中盈余公积金是有特定用途的累积盈余，未分配利润是没有指定用途的累积盈余。保留盈余的用途有三种：扩充营运规模，投资于新的企业，回购股票。

2. 普通股与优先股

普通股指的是在公司的经营管理和盈利及财产的分配上享有普通权利的股份,代表满足所有债权偿付要求及优先股东的收益权与求偿权要求后对企业盈利和剩余财产的索取权。它构成公司资本的基础,是股票的一种基本形式,也是发行量最大、最为重要的股票。

优先股是相对于普通股而言的,主要指在利润分红及剩余财产分配的权利方面优先于普通股。优先股股东没有选举及被选举权,一般来说对公司的经营没有参与权。优先股股东不能退股,其股份只能通过优先股的赎回条款被公司赎回,但是能稳定分红。

(1) 股利方面的区别。优先股有固定的股息,不随公司业绩好坏而波动,并且可以先于普通股股东领取股息;而普通股的股利收益没有上下限,视公司经营状况好坏、利润大小而定,公司税后利润在按一定的比例提取了公积金并支付优先股股息后,再按股份比例分配给普通股股东。

(2) 权利方面的区别。优先股的权利范围小,优先股股东一般没有选举权和被选举权,对股份公司的重大经营决策无投票权;普通股股东一般有出席股东大会的权利,有表决权、选举权和被选举权。

(3) 索偿权的区别。如果公司股东大会需要讨论与优先股有关的索偿权,那么优先股的索偿权先于普通股,次于债权人。

3. 现金股利与股票股利

现金股利是上市公司以货币形式支付给股东的股息红利,也是最普通、最常见的股利形式,如每股派息多少元,就是现金股利。股票股利是公司以增发股票的方式所支付的股利,通常也可被称为"红股"。

现金股利的发放致使公司的资产和股东权益减少同等数额,是企业资财的流出,会减少企业的可用资产,是利润的分配,是真正的股利。

股票股利是把原来股东所有的盈余公积转化为股东所有的投入资本,只不过不能再用来分派股利,实质上是留存利润的凝固化、资本化,不是真实意义上的股利。股票股利并不会导致资产从企业流出,发给股东的仅仅是其在公司的股东权益份额和价值。不管分不分股票股利,股东在公司里占有的权益份额和价值都不会变化。

如果用作股票股利的股票在证券市场上是热门股,股价坚挺,且作为股利新发行的股票不多,则可望股票市价并不因增发股票而有所下降,股票市价基本保持稳定,此时股东可将分得的股票股利在证券市场上抛售,换取现金利益。但这容易引起错觉:认为股票股利与现金股利无异,是实在股利。但这毕竟是假象,实际是通过拥有多一点股票来体现其在企业中的所有者权益份额情况,出售股票股利的股票就是出售股东在企业所拥有的权益。出售股票的所得，当然有可能包括一部分利润，也包括一部分投入资本。

4. 企业经营始终当以诚信为本

中华民族孕育了五千年的辉煌历史，滋养、造就了国人的良好品德。在历史的长河中，中华美德熠熠生辉，民族精神世代传承，其中诚信守诺更是文化瑰宝中的璀璨明珠。

中国历朝历代的统治者都将诚信守诺视为巩固江山的利器法宝，春秋时期的著名政治学家管仲在《管子·枢言》中讲道："先王贵诚信。诚信者，天下之结也。"孟子亦云："诚者，天之道也；思诚者，人之道也。"从中可以看出古人对于诚信的忠实程度。管理江山重视诚信，在现代社会中管理企业亦是如此。在现代经济领域中，诚信被看作无形资产，是市场秩序的支柱、经济繁荣的基石，可以说是企业立身之根本。中国共产党第二十次全国代表大会上也强调，构建高水平社会主义市场经济体制。完善产权保护、市场准入、公平竞争、社会信用等市场经济基础制度，优化营商环境。引入社会信用一词，一方面强调信用对于市场经济良性发展的重要性；另一方面指出社会信用对于构建社会主义全新发展格局起到推动作用。

本章中我们深入学习了所有者权益的构成、股票种类及股利发放的不同形式。我们应该意识到，作为企业的实际控制人，股东必须在遵纪守法、诚信守诺的前提下努力实现企业利润最大化的目标。

Exercises

1. Preferred stock owners have different rights from to common stockholders. Which one of the following is not the right of a preferred stock owner? (   )

    A. Receive a cash dividend.

    B. Voting rights.

    C. Liquidation preference.

    D. Participating.

2. On which date might you not record a journal entry for the outstanding stock? (   )

    A. Declaration date.

    B. Date of record.

    C. Payment date.

    D. None of the above.

3. SUNNY company issued 1,370,000 shares of stock on February 15, 2022. The total number of authorized shares is 3,200,000. The treasury stock repurchased by the company was 90,000 shares. How many unissued shares are there on the market? (　　)

　　A. 340,000 shares.　　　　　　　　B. 1,830,000 shares.
　　C. 1,740,000 shares.　　　　　　　D. 3,110,000 shares.

4. SUNNY company issued 1,660,000 shares of stock on February 15, 2022. The total number of authorized shares is 3,000,000. SUNNY company planned to issue the rest of shares (1,340,000 shares) in the second quarter. The treasury stock repurchased by the company was 100,000 shares. How many outstanding shares are there on the market? (　　)

　　A. 1240,000 shares.　　　　　　　B. 2,900,000 shares.
　　C. 1,440,000 shares.　　　　　　　D. 1,560,000 shares.

5. Which one of the following is false? (　　)

　　A. Authorized shares are the total number of shares that may legally be issued under the charter of incorporation.
　　B. Treasury stock is a corporation's issued stock that has subsequently been repurchased by the issuing company.
　　C. Outstanding shares are shares remaining in the hands of shareholders.
　　D. Issued stock represents the number of shares issued by the company on current date.

6. At liquidation, which kind of owners has the last liquidation preference? (　　)

　　A. Owners of unsubordinated debentures.
　　B. Owners of common stock.
　　C. Owners of subordinated debentures.
　　D. Owners of accounts payable.

7. Referring to the differences between bond and preferred stock, which one is not true among the following choices? (　　)

　　A. The bond interest reduces income before tax.
　　B. The preferred stock has an unlimited life.
　　C. The bond's return doesn't have to be paid to specific investors.
　　D. The cash dividend of preferred stock reduces net income and retained earnings directly.

8. A company paid large-percentage stock dividends to the shareholders on May 20. Which of the following accounts should the company credit? (　　)

　　A. Retained earnings.　　　　　　B. Common stock.
　　C. Cash dividend.　　　　　　　　D. Additional paid-in capital.

Stockholders' Equity Chapter 8

9. ECHO Ltd. issued small-percentage stock dividends. Which one of the following is the right journal entry? (   )

   A. Dr: common stock
       Cr: retained earnings (par value)

   B. Dr: common stock, additional paid-in capital
       Cr: retained earnings

   C. Dr: retained earnings (par value)
       Cr: common stock

   D. Dr: retained earnings
       Cr: common stock, additional paid-in capital

10. Which of the following is correct about stock dividends? (   )

    A. Stock dividends are distributions of cash to stockholders.

    B. Stock dividends have no effect on total stockholders' equity.

    C. Stock dividends reduce the total assets of the company.

    D. Stock dividends increase the corporation's total liabilities.

11. Wonka is a chocolate factory in the USA. Wonka started issuing its first common stock at NYSE on May 20, 2022. Assume Wonka issued 1,000,000 shares with par value of $8. The market price of the issued stock is $15. Prepare the journal entry.

12. In 2022, ChangCheng Company declared dividends of $0.5 per share for a total of 10 million shares. Assume the company declared dividends on September 1 of 2022, recorded stockholders on December 1, and distributed the dividends on December 20. Prepare the journal entries related to the necessary dates.

13. Suppose Ginsburg corporation declared and distributed a 30% stock dividend at par value $0.2 and market price of $5 to the shareholders with a total of 100,000 outstanding shares in 2022. Prepare the journal entries for this stock dividend distribution.

14. A clothing company named HEDY distributed a 4% stock dividend with a market price of $3 and par value of $1 to the shareholders on Dec. 21, 2022. Suppose that Mr. Hu, one of the company's shareholders, had 160 shares in total at that time. When the company distributed this stock dividend, how did Mr. Hu's stock change? Please show the calculation process and make a journal entry for this stock dividend distribution.

Chapter 9
Revenues and Expenses

Spotlight

Tom and Jerry just graduated from a business school in Sydney, and they planned to open a café in Sydney. They discovered a nice store at the corner of the street. The rent is relatively high because the store is located in a popular area. Their first big decision was whether to choose this store or not. After much consideration, they decided to rent the store, and planned to increase the price of each cup of coffee to cover the high rent. They thought the price was acceptable in Sydney. On January 1, 2022, their Express café opened after the renovation and preparation. After completing the above preparations, They will face more complex situations in daily activities. In this chapter, we will take Express café as an example to see how to record revenues and expenses. According to the income statement below, can you analyze the revenues and expenses of Express café?

EXHIBIT 9-1 is the income statement of Express café after one month of operation.

EXHIBIT 9-1 Income Statement of Express Café on December 31, 2022

Express Café Consolidated Statements of Earnings ($ in thousands) December 31, 2022	
Net Revenues:	
Net operating revenues	12,300
Other incomes and gains (net)	180
Total net revenue	12,480
Cost of sales	4,800
Store rent expenses	1,400
Other operating expenses	1,000
Depreciation expenses	450
General and administrative expenses	700
Other expenses	5
Income before income taxes	4,125
Income taxes expenses	1,650
Net income	2,475

Text

9.1 Accrual Basis and Cash Basis

For companies, the timing of revenue recognition is critical because it determines the final net income at the end of an accounting period. There are two main reasons for this: (1) it directly affects net income as it is one element of the accounting equation: net income equals revenues minus expenses; (2) it indirectly affects net income because it determines when a corporation records certain expenses. According to the matching principle, an enterprise records the cost of the items sold in the same accounting period in which the relevant revenue is recognized.

When we study the recognition of revenues or expenses, there are mainly two kinds of accounting basis: accrual basis and cash basis. The issue of revenue recognition is related to the business performance of the company, and has a greater impact on the accounting of the enterprise. Revenue recognition is a major problem in financial accounting. Whether and when the revenue can be recognized also depends on the professional judgment of the accountants.

9.1.1 Accrual Basis

Under the accrual basis, companies record transactions that will change a company's financial statements in the periods in which the events occur. Typically, a revenue is recognized when a critical event has occurred, when a product or service has been delivered to a customer, and the amount earned is easily measurable to the company. For example, using the accrual basis to determine the net income means companies recognize revenues when they perform services rather than when they receive cash. It also means that expenses were recognized when incurred rather than when paid.

9.1.2 Cash Basis

Under cash basis accounting, companies record revenues when they receive cash. They record an expense at the time when they pay out cash. The cash basis seems appealing due to its simplicity, but it often produces misleading financial statements. For example, it does not record the revenue for a company that has performed services but has not yet received payment. Therefore, the cash basis may not recognize the revenue in a period in which a performance obligation is satisfied.

9.2　Measurement of Sales Revenue

Revenue is money brought into a company by its business activities. The **sales revenue** is the total amount that is earned by the company, which includes **cash sales** as well as **credit sales**.

A cash sale means that cash is collected when the sale is made, and the goods or services are delivered to the customer. Accounting of cash sales is rather simple. A cash sale increases a company's sales revenue, which is an account in the income statement. It also increases cash, which is a balance sheet account.

A credit sale means that the company transfers the goods and services to the customers and allows the customers to pay for the goods and services later. When the goods are sold on credit to a buyer, the **accounts receivable** account debits, increasing the company's assets in the balance sheet. The corresponding credit will be in the sales revenue account, increasing the company's revenue.

Suppose Express café earned $2,000 cash on January 10, 2022. The journal entry for that day's revenue recognition would be:

Dr: Cash　　　　　　　　　　　　2,000
　　Cr: Sales revenue　　　　　　　2,000

In the meantime, the entity had a $500 of credit sale to be paid at the end of the month, in addition to the cash sales on January 10, 2022. The journal entry for such a transaction would then be different from cash sales.

Dr: Accounts receivable　　　　　　500
　　Cr: Sales revenue　　　　　　　500

9.3　Merchandise Returns and Allowances

Although recognizing sales revenue may seem straightforward, the amount of revenue recognized at the point of sale may differ from the amount of cash ultimately received. Sales returns and allowances account is used to describe the value of unsatisfactory merchandise returned by a customer or the value of a refund issued by a company to a customer. The sales returns and allowances account is shown in the company's income statement.

If a customer returned two bags of coffee beans to Express café because of the wrong flavor for a total of $70, the journal entry for this transaction would be:

Dr: Sales returns and allowances   70
    Cr: Cash   70

In another situation, when a customer is not satisfied with the goods, the seller offers to leave the goods to the customer at a reduced selling price. The buyer does not send the merchandise back to the seller but receives a reduction in the total amount that has to be paid to the seller for the order. For example, a customer was dissatisfied with the scratches on the coffee machine and asked for a reduction in the price of the coffee machine. Express café responded to this complaint by agreeing to give the customer a sales allowance.

Suppose there was a scratch on the coffee maker and the customer was offered a price reduction of $30. The journal entry for the sales allowance is:

Dr: Sales returns and allowances   30
    Cr: Cash   30

The two transactions above about the sale returns and allowances would affect the income statement as follows:

Gross sales	$2,000
Deduct: Sales returns and allowances	$100
Net sales	$1,900

The **sales returns and allowances account** is a contra-revenue account that is deducted from gross sales in the income statement. It is expected to have a debit balance instead of the usual credit balance. In other words, its expected balance is the opposite of the regular credit balance of the **sales revenue** account. Sales returns and allowances account is important for tracking the quality of products, assessing consumer satisfaction with the business, and analyzing the profitability of sales efforts.

9.4 Cash and Trade Discounts

Apart from sales returns and allowances, cash and trade discounts can also reduce original sales.

9.4.1 Trade Discounts

Trade discounts are reductions in price that a supplier offers to customers(usually on large-volume purchases). Trade discounts often state a particular amount. A corporation may offer discounts on total sales of merchandise over $100,000.

Suppose Express café holds a promotional activity—"three for the price of two". It means the customers can pay for 2 bags of coffee beans and get 1 bag for free. Because the price reduction occurs before the transaction, such recognition entries can be recorded directly at the discounted price without recording the original price.

9.4.2 Cash Discounts

Cash discounts are rewards that a seller offers to a buyer for prompt payment.

An example of a cash discount is as follows.

$n/30$	The full billed price (net price) is due on the 30th day after the invoice date.
$2/5, n/30$	A 2% discount can be taken for payment within 5 days of the invoice date; otherwise, the full billed price is due in 30 days.
30 EOM	End of the month (EOM) means that the payment is due in 30 days after the end of the month in which you sent the invoice. For example, if you and your customer agree to use 30 EOM and you invoice the customer on May 11, that payment will be due on June 30—in other words, 30 days after May 31.

On February 20, 2022, Express café sold 100 bags of coffee beans on credit to a customer for $2,800. The agreed payment date was February 27, 2022, one week later. Express café also offered the customer cash discounts of 1/4, n/7. The customer paid in full amount for the coffee beans on February 23, 2022. The journal entry would be as follows:

<u>On February 20, 2022</u>

Dr: Accounts receivable	2,800	
Cr: Sales revenue		2,800

<u>On February 23, 2022</u>

Dr: Cash	2,772	
Cash discounts	28	
Cr: Accounts receivable		2,800

9.5 Expenses

By far we have learned how to recognize revenues on the accrual basis. How about expenses? Expenses can be divided into two categories: (1) expenses related to the revenues earned that period; (2) expenses linked with the time period itself.

The first category usually refers to cost of goods sold. We recognize and record cost of goods sold in the same period in which we recognize revenue from related sales revenue.

Sometimes, it is difficult to tie some of the other expenses directly to specific revenues. For instance, rent expense is generally paid before the building is used, which is a prepaid expense for the company. One year's rent can benefit the company throughout the year, so the rent expense should be allocated to each month of the business. These expenses support the operation of the entity for a given period of time, and similar expenses include advertising expense, administrative expense, depreciation expense, and so forth. These expenses are called period costs. **Period costs** refer to all those costs which are not related or tied with the production process of the company. In other words, they are not assigned with any of the particular products of the company and are thus shown in the financial statement of the company for the accounting period in which they are incurred.

9.5.1 Expiration of Unexpired Costs

Prepaid expenses are incurred for assets that will be received at a later time. Prepaid expenses are payments made for goods or services that will be received in the future. Prepaid expenses are not recorded in an income statement initially. Instead, prepaid expenses are first recorded in the balance sheet; then, as the benefit of the prepaid expense is realized, or as the expense is incurred, it is recognized in the income statement. For instance, **prepaid rent** is an asset account in the balance sheet. Since the company consumes assets, such assets should be deducted from the balance and treated as an income statement expense. The main feature of unexpired cost is that past transactions create an asset and subsequent consumption is used to adjust the value of the asset. Other examples of prepaid expenses include prepaid insurance and office supplies inventory.

Express café rented a store on January 1, 2022 at $36,000,000 for the full year of 2022. This rent should be considered as a prepaid asset listed under current assets in the balance sheet. Because such expenses support the company for one year, after which the value of the asset declines over time, prepaid rent is transferred into expenses. The journal entry for this transaction and adjustment should be:

On January 1, 2022
  Dr: Prepaid rent   3,600,000
    Cr: Cash   3,600,000
Subsequent ending of months
  Dr: Rent expenses   300,000
    Cr: Prepaid rent   300,000

9.5.2 Accrual of Unrecorded Expenses

Wages can be a classic example of accrued expenses. An employee's salary is a liability that continues to grow as the employee performs his or her duties. It means that the accrued wages are incurred as employees provide services for the business.

Although the wages expenses increase hourly and daily, the accountants record these expenses only when preparing financial statements. Therefore, they make adjustments to update each accrued expense account at the end of the period before preparing the official financial statements. These adjustments are important in matching expenses to the exact period in which the revenues are generated.

- **Accounting for Payment of Wages**

Assume that employees of Express café can receive their salaries at the end of the month. Assume total monthly payroll expense is $12,000. How should the company record such transaction at the end of the month?

Dr: Wages expense   12,000
    Cr: Cash   12,000

- **Accounting for Accrual of Wages**

Suppose Express café paid employees salary on the 15th day of each month. Because the accountants prepare monthly financial statements, half of the wages have not yet been paid to the employees and become a liability in this way. If on June 30, 2022, Express café still owed its employees $6,000. The journal entry for this liability should be as follows:

Dr: Wages expense   6,000
    Cr: Accrued wages payable   6,000

In addition to accrual of wages, there are many similar accrued expenses such as **accrued interest payable, income taxes payable, and so on**. The journal entries for these transactions are similar to wages expenses.

Core Words

Revenues	收入
Expenses	费用
Matching	配比原则

Sales revenue	主营业务收入
Cost of sales/Cost of goods sold	主营业务成本
Cash discounts	现金折扣
Trade discounts	商业折扣
Credit sales	赊销
Cash sales	现销
Adjustments	期末调整
Depreciation expenses	折旧费用
Administrative expenses	管理费用
Period costs	期间费用
Prepaid expenses	预付账款
Accrued wages payable	应付职工薪酬
Accrued interest payable	应付利息
Accrued income tax payable	应交所得税费

Extended Reading

1. 配比原则

配比原则主要是指费用与收入的配比原则，一般在收入确定的情况下，将与该收入有关的费用挑出来进行配比，以计算当期的损益。配比原则是由权责发生制延伸出来的一个原则，该原则包含两个层次：一是因果关系配比，比如已销售手机的费用应该与手机销售收入进行配比，而不应该与卖电脑的收入进行配比；二是期间配比，有些费用的发生与某一具体收入不存在明显因果关系，比如广告费、办公费等，需要与发生在同一会计期间的收入进行配比。配比原则作为会计要素确认要求，用于利润确定。会计主体的经济活动会带来一定的收入，也必然要发生相应的费用。有所得必有所费，所费是为了所得，两者是对立的统一，利润正是所得比较所费的结果。配比原则的依据是受益原则，即谁受益，费用就归谁负担。受益原则承认得失之间存在因果关系，但并非所有费用与收入之间都存在因果关系，必须按照配比原则区分有因果联系的直接成本费用和没有直接联系的间接成本费用。直接费用与收入进行直接配比来确定本期损益；间接费用则通过判断采用适当合理的标准，先在各个产品和各期收入之间进行分摊，然后用收入配比来确定损益。

2. 现金折扣与商业折扣的区别

现金折扣是为鼓励客户提前付款而给予的债务扣除；现金折扣在商品销售后发生，企业在确认销售收入时不能确定相关的现金折扣，销售后现金折扣是否发生应视买方的付款情况而定；现金折扣是一种鼓励购买者快速支付其账单的价格削减方式，其期限在净期限内变更。例如，2/10，n/30 意思是如果在10天内付款，购买者能够从发票面值中得到2%的折扣。否则，在30天内支付全部金额。商业折扣是为促进销售而给予的价格扣除。商业折扣在销售时就已发生，企业销售实现时，按扣除商业折扣后的净额确认销售收入即可，不需要进行账务处理。

3. 期末账项调整

期末账项调整指在会计期末结账前，按权责发生制原则，正确划分各个会计期间应得收入和应负担的费用，为正确计算并结转本期经营成果提供相关资料，并对账簿记录的有关账项进行必要调整的会计处理方法。

4. 静以修身，俭以养德

诸葛亮在《诫子书》中说道："夫君子之行，静以修身，俭以养德，非淡泊无以明志，非宁静无以致远。"意思是恬静以修养身心，俭朴以培养品德。勤俭节约不是仅关系个人生活习惯和道德品行的小事，而是关乎社会风气和家国兴衰的大事。中华民族经历了从站起来、富起来到强起来的艰苦奋斗历程，但戒奢以俭的道理并未过时。我们要继续弘扬艰苦奋斗、勤俭节约的优秀传统，自觉养成勤俭节约的习惯，让厉行节约、反对铺张浪费的风尚继续引领我们奔向更美好的生活。

为在全社会营造浪费可耻、节约为荣的氛围，使厉行勤俭节约、反对铺张浪费成为教师、学生的自觉行动，多所高校开展"光盘行动"，切实强化引导，培养学生勤俭节约的美德，杜绝舌尖上的浪费。长安大学响应"光盘行动，为爱捐餐"倡议，推出"光盘打卡"活动。学生通过网络扫码的方式进入"光盘打卡"小程序，由AI识别是否光盘，打卡成功后即可获得正能量，它可用于支持希望厨房公益项目。为让同学们养成勤俭节约的好习惯，青岛农业大学开展光盘行动，引导大学生节粮、节水、节电，使"三节"教育不断深入人心。赣南师范大学北苑心怡餐厅推出"光盘行动兑饭票"的活动，鼓励广大同学提高节约意识，从点滴做起，逐渐培养节约资源的良好习惯，让人人都争做"资源节约使者"。

勤俭节约、艰苦奋斗是中华民族的重要文化传统和民族精神，也是我们党不断取得事业胜利的重要法宝。经过千百年的发展，勤俭节约、艰苦奋斗已经成为一种精神、一种品格、一种作风、一种象征。随着时代和实践的发展，它还在不断地被赋予新的内涵。在改革开放和发展社会主义市场经济的条件下，节俭意识和艰苦奋斗精神的具体内涵与过去相比有所不同，但尊重劳动、物尽其用、自强不息、顽强拼搏仍然是其要义，是我们必须始终坚持和弘扬的。对于大学生而言，树立节俭意识和坚持艰苦奋斗精神，主要是养成艰苦朴素、勤俭节约的生活作风，树立奋发向上、自强不息的人生态度，弘扬埋头苦干、知难而进的进取精神。学生要树立勤俭节约意识，学会科学消费、绿色消费。大学生要牢固树立艰苦奋斗的事业观、价值观和生活观，自觉抵制享乐主义和奢靡之风，鼓励勤俭节约，践行勤俭节约，尊重劳动人民的劳动成果，扎实做好厉行节约工作。

Exercises

1. Which of the following statements about revenues is correct? ( )

    A. Revenues decrease in liabilities due to loan repayments.

    B. Revenues increase in retained earnings because of selling products or providing services to consumers.

    C. Revenues decrease in paid-in capital due to investor investment in the business.

    D. All of the above.

2. It is very important to account for the timing of revenue recognition, because (   ).

    A. it affects the net income directly

    B. it has impact on the net income indirectly

    C. it also affects the recognition of related expenses

    D. all of the above

3. Under IFRS, accounting is based on (   ).

    A. cash basis

    B. auditing basis

    C. accrual basis

    D. asset basis

4. If a corporation made a credit sale to a customer for $300,000, which of the following is the correct journal entry? (   )

    A. Debit cash.
    B. Debit accounts receivable.
    C. Credit depreciation expense.
    D. Credit notes payable.

5. Suppose the customer was not satisfied with the product's quality because there were some visible flaws on it. The customer wanted a price reduction of $20. Which of the following journal entries is correct? (   )

    A. Debit accounts receivable.
    B. Debit accounts payable.
    C. Credit sales returns and allowances.
    D. Credit cash.

6. Which of the following situations does not require a new journal entry to record allowances or discounts? (   )

    A. Sales returns.
    B. Sales allowances.
    C. Trade discount.
    D. Cash discount.

7. A company made a credit sale for $2,000 on February 1, 2022. The company gave the customer a cash discount of 1/4, n/7. The customer paid in full amount within three days. The journal entry for this payment should be (   )

    A. Debit: Cash
        Credit: Cash discount and accounts receivable
    B. Debit: Cash discount
        Credit: Accounts receivable and sales return
    C. Debit: Accounts receivable
        Credit: Cash and trade discount
    D. None of the above.

8. A company made a credit sale for $2,000 on February 1, 2022. The company gave the customer a cash discount of 1/4, n/7. The customer paid in full amount within three days. How much cash did the company receive after the customer's payment? (   )

    A. 0.
    B. $2,000.
    C. $20.
    D. $1,980.

9. Which of the following statements is false? (   )

    A. Period costs refer to all those costs which are not related or tied with the production process of the company.
    B. Prepaid rent is an asset account in the balance sheet.

C. Trade discounts can be recorded directly at the discounted price without recording the original price.

D. None of the above.

10. Which of the following statements is false?（   ）

A. Sales revenue account is usually recognized as cash sales or credit sales.

B. In addition to returns and allowances, cash and trade discounts also reduce original sales.

C. Sales returns and allowances account is a contra-revenue account that is deducted from gross sales in the income statement.

D. None of the above.

11. What are the differences between cash discounts and trade discounts?

12. Revenue recognition, cash discounts, and returns.

On February 19, 2022, ABC Products sold 1,000 items to a customer at $50 per item. The goods arrived on February 24, when ABC Products sent a bill to the customer for payment. ABC Products would give a 2% cash discount if the customer could pay within 10 days. The customer paid in full on February 28, 2022. However, on March 9, the customer returned 60 units for a full cash refund.

Prepare the entries for (1) February 19, (2) February 24, (3) February 28 and (4) March 9.

13. Make journal entries for the following transactions:

(1) The company sold goods with credit sales of $30,000 and cash sales of $10,000. The cost of inventory was $20,000.

(2) The company recognized $9,500 rent expense for this month.

(3) The company recognized $1,000 insurance expense for this month.

(4) The company returned part of the inventory which was valued at $5,000.

(5) The customer asked for a reduction of $50 because of the poor color of the product.

(6) The company sold 10,000 pencils for $3 each and gave a trade discount of $2 to customers who bought more than 1,000 units.

Chapter 10

Financial Statements

Spotlight

Sunny and her friends just graduated from an Australian fashion design school as undergraduates. They opened a clothing store called Rosemary. Through consulting some accountants, they learned that regular analysis of financial data was essential to the health of a business. The accountants emphasized that maintaining correct financial statements could help you determine the financial condition of your business at a specific point in time.

Information from the accounting journal and the general ledger is used to prepare the financial statements of a business. Income statement, the statement of retained earnings, balance sheet, and the statement of cash flow are the main types of financial statements. Regularly updating financial statements help a company grow, prepare for the future, and better determine its capital needs.

Through the accountants' explanation, Sunny and her friends had a preliminary understanding of the financial statements. As a student learning accounting, do you know the format requirements of financial statements, how to prepare financial statements, and how to interpret financial statements? Accountants prepare financial statements that can be shown to a company's owners so that the owners can get a clear picture of the company's financial position and business performance. What other parties use the company's financial statements, and why?

Text

10.1 Overview of Financial Statements

A financial statement (or financial report) is a formal record of the financial activities and position of a business, person, or other entities.

In a financial statement, relevant financial information is presented in a structured manner and in a form that is easy to understand.

A balance sheet (or statement of financial position) reports on a company's assets, liabilities, and owners' equity at a certain point of time.

An income statement (or statement of comprehensive income, statement of revenue & expense, P&L, or profit and loss report) reports on a company's income, expenses, and profits over a period of time. A profit and loss statement provides information on the operation of an enterprise. This includes sales and the various expenses incurred during the stated period.

A statement of changes in equity (or equity statement, or statement of retained earnings) reports on the changes in the equity of a company during the stated period.

A cash flow statement reports on a company's cash flow activities, particularly its operating, investing, and financing activities.

For large corporations, these statements may be complex and may include an extensive set of footnotes. The notes typically describe each item in the balance sheet, income statement, and cash flow statement in further detail. Notes are considered to be an integral part of the financial statements.

Stakeholders need to obtain information about the business to make the right decisions. The financial statement is the tool for them to get information.

There are four main kinds of financial statements:

- Income statement.
- Statement of retained earnings.
- Balance sheet.
- Statement of cash flow.

What would stakeholders want to know about a company? How can we obtain information from these financial statements? The role of each financial statement is shown in EXHIBIT 10-1.

EXHIBIT 10-1 Information from the Financial Statements

Question	Financial Statement	Answer
What's the performance of a company during the year?	Income statement	Revenues−Expenses
Why did the retained earnings change?	Statement of retained earnings	Beginning retained earnings+Net income (−Net loss) −Dividends
What's the financial position at the end of the year?	Balance sheet	Assets=Liabilities+Stockholders' equity

		(Continued)
Question	Financial Statement	Answer
What's the status of cash flow during the year?	Statement of cash flow	Operating cash flow±Investing cash flow±Financing cash flow= Increase (decrease) in cash

10.2　Formats for Financial Statements

10.2.1　Income Statement Formats

- **Single-step Income Statement**

In a single-step format, all the revenues are listed together under a heading, such as revenues. All the expenses are listed together under a heading, such as expenses. There is only one step to calculate the net income (or net loss). A single-step income statement is shown in EXHIBIT 10-2.

EXHIBIT 10-2　Single-step Income Statement

Income Statement March 31, 2022 ($ in thousands)	
Revenues:	
Net operation revenues	7,785
Other incomes	89
Total net revenues	7,876
Expenses:	
Cost of goods sold	3,179
Store operating expenses	2,688
Other operating expenses	260
Depreciation expenses	387
Administrative expenses	473
Total operating expenses	6,987
Income before income taxes	889
Income tax expense	325
Net income	562

- **Multi-step Income Statement**

In a multi-step income statement, there is no heading like revenues or expenses. Instead, gross profit, income from operations, income before tax, and net income are highlighted for emphasis. A multi-step income statement is shown in EXHIBIT 10-3.

Financial Statements Chapter 10

EXHIBIT 10-3 Multi-step Income Statement

Income Statement
March 31, 2022
($ in thousands)

Net operation revenues		7,785
Cost of goods sold		3,179
Gross profit		4,680
Store operating expenses	2,688	
Other operating expenses	260	
Depreciation expenses	387	
Administrative expenses	473	
Total operating expense		3,808
Income from operations		800
Other incomes		89
Income before income taxes		889
Income tax expense		325
Net income		562

10.2.2 Balance Sheet Formats

- **Report Format Balance Sheet**

The report format lists the assets at the top, followed by the liabilities and stockholders' equity. A report format balance sheet is shown in EXHIBIT 10-4.

EXHIBIT 10-4 Report Format Balance Sheet

Balance Sheet
December 31, 2022
($ in thousands)

Assets

Current assets:	
Cash and cash equivalents	311
Short-term investments	145
Accounts receivable	245
Inventories	622
Other current assets	211
Total current assets	1,534
Long-term investments	225
Property, plant, and equipment, net	2,288
Intangible assets	199
Other assets	165
Total assets	4,411

(Continued)

Balance Sheet
December 31, 2022
($ in thousands)

Liabilities and Stockholders' Equity	
Current liabilities:	
Accounts payable	450
Short-term notes payable	980
Total current liabilities	1,430
Long-term debts	2
Other long-term liabilities	68
Total liabilities	1,500
Stockholders' equity:	
Common stock	500
Retained earnings	2,000
Other equity	411
Total stockholders' equity	2,911
Total liabilities and shareholders' equity	4,411

- **Account Format Balance Sheet**

In an account format balance sheet, the assets are on the left, and the liabilities and stockholders' equity are on the right, just like items in a T-account.

An account format balance sheet is shown in EXHIBIT 10-5.

EXHIBIT 10-5 Account Format Balance Sheet

Balance Sheet
December 31, 2022
($ in thousands)

Assets		Liabilities	
Current assets:		Current liabilities:	
Cash and cash equivalents	311	Accounts payable	450
Short-term investments	145	Short-term notes payable	980
Accounts receivable	245	Total current liabilities	1,430
Inventories	622	Long-term debts	2
Other current assets	211	Other long-term liabilities	68
Total current assets	1,534	Total liabilities	1,500
Long-term investments	225	**Stockholders' Equity:**	
Property, plant, and equipment, net	2,288	Common stock	500
Intangible assets	199	Retained earnings	2,000
Other assets	165	Other equity	411
Total assets	4,411	Total stockholders' equity	2,911
		Total liabilities and shareholders' equity	4,411

Financial Statements — Chapter 10

Financial statements are related and compiled in order. The relationship is shown in EXHIBIT 10-6.

EXHIBIT 10-6 Relationship of the Financial Statements

Income Statement
December 31, 2021
($ in thousands)

Revenues:		
Service revenues		330
Expenses:		
Salary expense	177	
Depreciation expense—equipment	20	
Depreciation expense—building	10	
Supplies expense	4	
Miscellaneous expense	13	224
Income before income taxes		106
Income tax expense		35
Net income		71

Statement of Retained Earnings
December 31, 2021
($ in thousands)

Retained earnings, December 31, 2020	193
Add: Net income	71
	264
Less: Dividends	(65)
Retained earnings, December 31, 2021	199

Balance Sheet
December 31, 2021
($ in thousands)

Assets			Liabilities	
Cash		198	Accounts payable	380
Accounts receivable		382	Salary payable	5
Supplies		2	Unearned service revenue	13
Equipment	100		Income tax payable	35
Less: Accumulated depreciation	(60)	40	Total liabilities	433
Building	250		**Stockholders' Equity**	
Less: Accumulated depreciation	(140)	110	Common stock	100
Total assets		732	Retained earnings	199
			Total stockholders' equity	299
			Total liabilities and stockholders' equity	732

The order to prepare financial statements:

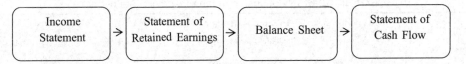

Core Words

Income statement	利润表
Statement of retained earnings	留存收益表
Balance sheet	资产负债表
Statement of cash flow	现金流量表
Single-step income statement	单步式利润表
Multi-step income statement	多步式利润表
Report format balance sheet	报告式资产负债表
Account format balance sheet	账户式资产负债表

Extended Reading

1. 财务报表

财务报表是以会计准则为规范编制的，向所有者、债权人、政府及其他有关各方及社会公众等外部反映会计主体财务状况和经营成果的会计报表。

财务报表包括资产负债表、利润表、现金流量表、附表和附注。财务报表是财务报告的主要部分。

资产负债表反映企业资产、负债及资本的期末状况，还反映企业的长期偿债能力、短期偿债能力和利润分配能力等。

利润表又称损益表。它反映企业本期收入、费用和应该计入当期利润的利得和损失的金额和结构情况。

现金流量表反映企业现金流量的来龙去脉，分为经营活动、投资活动及筹资活动三部分。

所有者权益变动表反映本期企业所有者权益总量的增减变动情况以及结构变动情况，特别是反映直接计入所有者权益的利得和损失。

财务报表附注一般包括如下项目：企业的基本情况、财务报表编制基础、遵循企业会计准则的声明、重要的会计政策和会计估计、会计政策和会计估计变更及差错的更正说明和重要的报表项目说明。

2. 关于财务报表的中外差异

在我国，企业的利润表采用多步式进行编制，资产负债表采用账户式进行编制，而国际会计准则中没有明确的要求。以美国为例，企业可以自主选择使用单步式或多步式对利润表进行列报，也可以根据企业自身需要混合使用单步式和多步式。同样，企业也可以自主选择采用报告式或账户式对资产负债表进行编制。

另外，对于所有者权益的披露，我国企业编制的是所有者权益变动表，而美国企业则编制留存收益表。

3. 财务共享中心对企业财务会计的影响

财务共享中心是近年来流行起来的会计核算管理方式。它将不同国家、地点的实体会计业务拿到一个共享服务中心来记账和报告，可以保证会计记录和报告的规范、结构统一，而且由于不需要在每个公司和办事处都设会计，能节省系统和人工成本。财务共享中心的主要职能是整合企业的基础财务业务，使子公司与分支机构和总公司的联系得以不断加强，通过实时的交流，使各个分部的财务会计工作得以顺利完成。

在财务管理实践中，依托于大数据技术及信息技术，财务共享模式成为现阶段的主流模式，也成为企业发展的主要方向。财务共享中心直接影响企业会计人员的职能和工作内容。在财务共享中心的影响下，会计人员机械化的会计核算及会计记录等工作职能逐步弱化，相反，会计的管理职能更加突出。企业的财务机构将随着财务共享中心的构建发生较大的改变，企业只需要较少的财务人员便可以完成会计记录和核算工作。企业将需要更多的具有战略眼光和拥有多方面知识的财务人员。财务共享中心要求不同会计人员分别扮演不同的角色，继而全方位提升财务管理工作的整体成效。财务人员要具备全面、专业的财务知识，并且具备战略发展眼光，了解财务相关知识，并且具有良好的管理能力。此外，财务人员还需要具有良好的沟通能力，与企业各业务部门进行沟通，从而从财务的角度对公司的资源进行合理的配置，最终优化企业的业务结构。

中国境内的企业财务共享服务正在步入快速发展的阶段，在未来，大量的集团企业将建立财务共享服务中心模式。企业通过财务共享转型后，单一功能的财会人员将不能满足企业需求。对业务充分了解并能参与企业经营管理的复合型财务人员才是企业之所需。面对财务共享和人工智能的发展，财会专业的大学生应该构建综合的知识体系，注重理论和实践的结合，永远保持主动学习的态度。科技的发展和知识的更新要求在校大学生不断加强自身建设，满足就业市场对高技能人才的需求，让未来就业的道路更加通畅。

Exercises

1. Which of the following is included in gross profit? (　　)
   A. Cost of goods sold.　　　B. Operating expense.
   C. Depreciation expense.　　D. Administrative expense.

2. Which of the following will not affect the operating expense? (　　)
   A. Depreciation expense.　　B. Administrative expense.
   C. Cost of goods sold.　　　D. Rent expense.

3. Which one of the following is the most liquid current asset? (　　)
   A. Cash and cash equivalents.　B. Short-term investment.
   C. Accounts receivable.　　　D. Inventory.

4. Which one of the following is a long-term asset? (　　)
   A. Inventory.　　　　　B. Accounts receivable.
   C. Investment.　　　　D. Intangibles.

5. What is included in the statement of cash flow? (　　)
   A. Operating cash flow.　　B. Investing cash flow.
   C. Financing cash flow.　　D. All of the above.

6. What is the right order of accounting work? (　　)
   A. Ledger, journal, trial balance, financial statement.
   B. Journal, ledger, trial balance, financial statement.
   C. Financial statement, ledger, journal, trial balance.
   D. Journal, trial balance, ledger, financial statement.

7. What is the right order to prepare financial statements? (　　)
   A. Income statement, statement of retained earnings, balance sheet, statement of cash flow.
   B. Income statement, balance sheet, statement of retained earnings, statement of cash flow.

C. Balance sheet, income statement, statement of retained earnings, statement of cash flow.

D. Statement of cash flow, income statement, statement of retained earnings, balance sheet.

8. **Which of the following is reported in paid-in capital account? (   )**
   A. Dividend.   B. Administrate expense.
   C. Preferred stock.   D. Cash and cash equivalents.

9. **Which of the following appears on both a single-step and a multi-step income statement? (   )**
   A. Sales.   B. Operating income.
   C. Gross profit.   D. Cost of goods sold.

10. **Which of the following is the investing activity of statement of cash flow? (   )**
    A. Payment of cash to suppliers for inventory.
    B. Payment of cash to purchase outstanding capital stock.
    C. Receipt of cash from the issuance of bonds payable.
    D. Receipt of cash from the sale of equipment.

11. **Identify the 2 basic categories of items in an income statement.**

12. **What do we call the bottom line of the income statement?**

13. Identify the 2 basic categories of items in a balance sheet.

Chapter 11
Auditing

Spotlight

The word "audit" is derived from a Latin word "audire" which means "to hear". During Medieval Times when manual bookkeeping was prevalent, auditors in Britain used to hear the accounts read out for them and check whether or not the organization's personnel were negligent or fraudulent. Moyer identified that the most important duty of the auditor was to detect fraud. Chatfield documented that in early America, auditing was mainly viewed as verification of bookkeeping details.

An external auditor performs an audit, in accordance with specific laws or rules, of the financial statements of a company, government entity, other legal entities, or organizations, and is independent of the entity being audited. Users of these entities' financial information, such as investors, government agencies, and the general public, rely on the external auditor to present an unbiased and independent audit report.

The manner of appointment, the qualifications, and the format of reporting by an external auditor are defined by the statute, which varies according to jurisdiction. External auditors must be members of one of the recognized professional accountancy bodies. External auditors normally address their reports to the shareholders of a corporation. In the United States, certified public accountants are the only authorized non-governmental external auditors who may perform audits and attestations on an entity's financial statements and provide reports on such audits for public review.

For public companies listed on stock exchanges in the United States, the Sarbanes-Oxley Act has imposed stringent requirements on external auditors in their evaluation of internal controls and financial reporting. In many countries, external auditors of nationalized commercial entities are appointed by an independent government body such as the Comptroller and Auditor General. Securities and Exchange Commissions may also impose specific requirements and roles on external auditors, including strict rules to establish independence.

Text

11.1 Audit Framework

11.1.1 Necessity of Auditing

With the development of the market economy, the ownership and management of enterprises are gradually separated. The owner no longer participates in the management of the enterprise. So how do shareholders understand the day-to-day operations of the business? They can get information from the financial statements. However, there is a conflict in this process. Directors are in charge of the management of an entity as well as preparing the financial statements of this entity. External audits can ensure that financial statements are objective, free from bias and manipulation, and relevant to the needs of the users who will review the financial statements. External audits can help to protect shareholders' interest.

11.1.2 Nature of Audit

According to ISA 200, the purpose of an audit is to enhance the degree of confidence of intended users in the financial statements. This is achieved by the expression of an opinion by the auditor on whether the financial statements are prepared, in all material respects, in accordance with an applicable financial reporting framework.

Auditors do not certify the financial statements or guarantee that the financial statements are correct. They only give a reasonable assurance that the information audited is free of material misstatement.

11.1.3 Advantages of Audit

External auditors are completely independent of the business. They are hired to determine whether the company's financial statements comply with generally accepted accounting principles. Auditors examine the clients' financial statements and the underlying transactions in order to form a professional opinion of the financial statements. The advantages of audit can be summarized as follows.

Disputes among the managerial personnel are easier to resolve. This is because the audit helps to provide an independent examination of the financial statements. Therefore, the report on the results of the operation is more reliable.

Major changes in the ownership may be facilitated if the past accounts contain an unqualified auditing report.

Auditing can help an entity to find problems in their previous job, and to give constructive advice to the management on improving the efficiency of the business.

Auditing can help third parties like tax department and banks obtain more fair information.

11.1.4　Disadvantages of Audit

The disadvantages of audit can be summarized as follows:

(1) The audit will bring fees. It is worth noting that auditing does not help companies improve profits. On the contrary, auditing produces fees.

(2) The audit will affect the normal working schedule of the enterprise. The audit involves the client's staff and management in providing information to the auditor. A professional auditor should therefore plan the audit procedure carefully to minimize the disruption.

11.1.5　Stages of Audit

- **Planning Stage**

There are two main substances in the planning process. One is to compile the annual audit project plan. Another is to compile the audit work plan, which mainly includes the audit target, scope, content, and emphasis.

- **Audit Implementation Stage**

(1) Interim Audit. It is carried out during the period of review. The work tends to focus on **risk assessment** and on documenting and testing **internal control.** Some substantive procedures can also be carried out but these are limited.

(2) Final Audit. It focuses on the audit of the financial statements and concludes with the auditor issuing a report.

- **Reporting Stage**

It is the final stage when the auditor expresses an opinion on the financial statements.

11.2 Professional Ethics and Codes of Conduct

Ethics are about what is morally wrong or right. The code of ethics is not a legal requirement but it is advisable to follow. Why?

- It increases the user's confidence that the auditor is functioning according to a code of ethics.
- The auditors need the code of ethics to make sure that they are worthy of trust.
- The rules can help to uphold the level and quality of work performed.
- The rules deter people from violating ethical codes.
- If the code of ethics is not applied, disciplinary actions may be taken.
- The maintenance of professional codes of ethics helps the accounting personnel act in the public interest by providing appropriate regulations.

11.2.1 Fundamental Principles

- **Integrity**

Members should be straightforward and honest in all professional/business relationships. It's not allowed to provide false, misleading, or incomplete information.

- **Objectivity**

Members do not allow bias or conflict of interest in business judgments. Conflict of interest and influences should be avoided.

- **Professional Competence and Due Care**

A professional accountant should maintain professional knowledge and skills at the level required to ensure that a client or an employer receives competent professional service based on current developments in practice, legislation, and techniques, and act diligently and in accordance with applicable, technical, and professional standards.

- **Confidentiality**

Information on clients should not be disclosed without appropriate specific authority.

- **Professional Behavior**

Members should comply with relevant laws and avoid actions discrediting the profession.

11.2.2 Independence

Independence is the cornerstone of the auditing profession.

Why is it necessary for external auditors to be independent?

Here are some reasons:

(1) Agency theory: Because they act on behalf of the owners (shareholders) and report on the financial statements prepared by the appointed management staff for the benefit of the shareholders.

(2) Statute: National legislation requires it.

(3) The ACCA rules of professional conduct require that auditors are independent and they are seen to be independent. The rules cover a number of areas in which auditors' independence may be or be seen to be impaired.

(4) Auditors must be seen to be independent because if they are not independent, the owners of the business will not have confidence in the audit report that they issue.

The key point is independence in terms of appearance and mind.

- **Independence of mind**

It is the state of mind that permits the expression of an opinion without being affected by influences that compromise professional judgment, allowing an individual to act with integrity, and exercise objectivity and professional skepticism.

- **Independence in appearance**

It is the avoidance of facts and circumstances that are so significant that a reasonable and informed third party would be likely to conclude, weighing all the specific facts and circumstances, that a firm's, or a member of the audit team's, integrity, objectivity, or professional skepticism has been compromised.

11.2.3　Threats to Independence

(1) Self-interest threat: It occurs when the auditor's financial or other interests are involved.

(2) Self-review threat: It occurs when the auditor has to evaluate the work again which was completed by himself.

(3) Advocacy threat: It occurs when the auditor is asked to promote the clients' position or represent them in some way.

(4) Familiarity threat: It occurs when the auditor is too sympathetic or trusting of the clients because of a close relationship with them.

(5) Intimidation threat: It occurs when the auditor is intimidated to give an unqualified opinion or otherwise he would not be re-appointed.

11.3 Standards of Reporting

(1) The report should state whether the financial statements are presented in accordance with generally accepted accounting principles.

(2) The report should identify those circumstances in which such principles have not been consistently observed in the current period in relation to the preceding period.

(3) Informative disclosures in the financial statements are to be regarded as reasonably adequate unless otherwise stated in the report.

(4) The report should either contain an expression of opinion regarding the financial statements, taken as a whole, or an assertion to the effect that an opinion cannot be expressed. When an overall opinion cannot be expressed, the reasons therefore should be stated. In all cases where an auditor's name is associated with the financial statements, the report should contain a clear-cut indication of the character of the auditor's work (if any) and the degree of responsibility the auditor is taking.

11.3.1 Unqualified Opinions

An unqualified opinion states that the auditors followed generally accepted auditing standards in the conduct of the audit and that in their opinion the financial statements are fairly presented in accordance with generally accepted accounting principles.

However, some conditions may prevent the auditors from completely following generally accepted auditing standards or the auditors may find something during the course of the audit that prevents them from reporting that the financial statements are fair in all respects. In such a case, one of three types of reports other than "unqualified" is issued: (1) a qualified opinion, (2) a disclaimer, or (3) an adverse opinion.

11.3.2 Qualified Opinions

A qualified opinion states that, with the exception of the qualification or qualifications noted, generally accepted auditing standards were followed and the financial statements are fairly presented in conformity with generally accepted accounting principles. Basically, there are two reasons for which auditors might issue a qualified opinion.

Firstly, some circumstances might prevent them from performing all the audit procedures necessary to follow generally accepted auditing standards. For example, the auditors may not be on hand to observe the count of inventory quantities conducted by the client. If inventory represents a significant portion of total assets (as it often does), the auditors may have to issue a qualified opinion because of the inadequate scope of their audit.

Secondly, during the course of the audit, the auditors may conclude that certain accounting techniques followed by the client are not in accordance with generally accepted accounting principles or that all proper informative disclosures have not been made in the financial statements. In other words, the auditors have conducted the audit in accordance with generally accepted auditing standards and have found omissions or discrepancies that require a qualified opinion.

11.3.3 Disclaimers

A disclaimer states that the scope of the audit is so inadequate that the auditors do not render any opinion on the financial statements, or an uncertainty might have such a serious potential impact on the financial statements that the auditors refuse to give an opinion. The applicable report in these circumstances is one that disclaims an opinion on the financial statements and gives the reasons for doing so. A disclaimer in an auditor's report can have a serious impact on readers' views of the accompanying financial statements. This type of report is therefore rendered only if the auditors are convinced that the inadequate scope or the uncertainty is too serious to warrant a qualified opinion.

11.3.4 Adverse Opinions

An adverse opinion states that, as the result of audit evidence, the auditor concludes that the financial statements taken as a whole are not fairly stated in conformity with generally accepted accounting principles. For example, such a conclusion might be formed because the client records a significant amount of its fixed assets at appraisal value rather than cost.

An adverse opinion, like a disclaimer of opinion, can have a serious effect on the views of readers of the accompanying financial statements. Such an opinion would be issued by the auditors only if they believe that the deviation from generally accepted accounting principles is too serious to warrant a qualified opinion.

The standards of audit opinions are listed in EXHIBIT 11-1.

EXHIBIT 11-1　Standards of Audit Opinions

Nature of matter giving rise to the modification	Auditor's judgment about the pervasiveness of the effects or possible effects on the financial statements	
	Material but not pervasive	Material and pervasive
Financial statements are materially misstated	Qualified opinion	Adverse opinion
Auditor unable to obtain sufficient appropriate audit evidence	Qualified opinion	Disclaimer of opinion

Core Words

Planning stage	审计计划阶段
Audit implementation stage	审计实施阶段
Reporting stage	审计报告阶段
Risk assessment	风险评估
Internal control	内部控制
Integrity	真实性
Objectivity	客观性
Professional competence and due care	职业能力和适当关注
Confidentiality	保密性
Professional behavior	职业行为
Independence	独立性
Independence of mind	实质上的独立性
Independence in appearance	形式上的独立性
Unqualified opinions	无保留意见
Qualified opinions	保留意见
Disclaimers	无法发表审计意见
Adverse opinions	反对意见

Extended Reading

1. 审计的定义

审计是由国家授权或接受委托的专职机构人员依照国家法规、审计准则和会计准则，运用专门的方法，对被审计单位的财政、财务支出、经营管理活动及其相关资料的真实性、正确性、合规性、合法性、效益性进行审查和监督，评价经济责任，鉴证经济业务，用于维护财经法纪、改善经营管理、提高经济效益的一项独立性的经济监督活动。

2. 审计的分类

按审计活动执行主体的性质分类，审计可以分为政府审计(government audit)、独立审计(independent audit)、内部审计(internal audit)三种。本章介绍的审计指的是外部审计(external audit)，也就是独立审计。

3. 审计意见的类型

1) 标准的无保留意见(unmodified opinion)
审计师认为被审计者编制的财务报表已按照适用的会计准则的规定编制并在所有重大方面公允反映了被审计者的财务状况、经营成果和现金流量。

2) 带有强调事项段的无保留意见(unmodified opinion with an emphasis of matter paragraph)
审计师认为被审计者编制的财务报表符合相关会计准则的要求并在所有重大方面反映了被审计者的财务状况、经营成果和现金流量，但是存在需要说明的事项，如对持续经营能力产生重大疑虑及重大不确定事项。

3) 保留意见(qualified opinion)
审计师认为财务报表整体是公允的，但是存在影响重大的错报。

4) 否定意见(adverse opinion)
审计师认为财务报表整体是不公允的或没有按照适用的会计准则的规定编制。

5) 无法发表意见(disclaimer of opinion)
审计师的审计范围受到了限制，且其可能产生的影响是重大而广泛的，审计师不能获取充分的审计证据。

4. 强调事项段

审计报告的强调事项段是指注册会计师在审计意见段之后增加的对重大事项予以强调的段落。强调事项段应同时符合下列条件:

(1) 可能对财务报表产生重大影响,但被审计单位进行了恰当的会计处理,且在财务报表中予以充分披露。

(2) 不影响注册会计师发表审计意见。

5. 遵纪守法,廉洁自律

纪律是我们必须遵守的行为规则。过去,纪律是我们革命制胜的法宝,现在,它是我们事业取得成功的保证。我们身处任何环境,做任何事时都要遵守纪律,受纪律的约束。

公孙仪谈吃鱼的故事相信大家都知道。公孙仪在鲁国做宰相,他非常喜欢吃鱼。在他任职期间,许多人买了鱼给他送礼,可是公孙仪从不收。"老师,您不是很喜欢吃鱼吗?"公孙仪的学生笑着问公孙仪,"现在有这么多人给您送鱼,您都不接受,这是为什么呢?"公孙仪说:"正因为我喜欢吃鱼,所以才不收人家的鱼。如果我收了人家的礼,就要照人家的意见办事,这就难免要犯国家的法纪,一个正直的人不应该这样做。试想,如果我犯了法,就成了罪人,鱼也吃不成了。现在爱吃鱼就自己去买,不是一直可以吃到鱼吗?"

这个故事千百年来广为传颂,其中的道理,不言而喻。审计人员经常和被审计对象打交道,不能因为自己一时的欲望就违背原则,触犯法律法规,不然,执法就有失公正。我们必须在法律允许的范围内开展工作,说话办事处处维护审计的形象和尊严。每个审计人员手中都有"自由裁量权",用好了,有益社会、人民,用不好,为自己"造罪"。作为审计人员,我们要时刻有如临深渊、如履薄冰的感觉,做到心存敬畏,警钟长鸣。要学会正确比较,努力排除各种权、钱、利等因素的干扰,客观公正地开展审计工作。

我们要把握底线标准,自筑"防火墙",自设"高压线"。要做到不该做的不做,不该拿的不拿,不该去的地方不去。要筑牢思想防线,不断加强世界观的改造。时刻保持清醒的头脑,大事不糊涂,小事讲原则,要常思贪欲之害,常怀律己之心。

Exercises

1. Which of the following statements is false? (　　)

    A. External audit can also be called independent audit.

    B. The purpose of auditing is to guarantee that there is no error in financial statements.

    C. Auditing cannot help a company to improve profits.

    D. The audit will affect the normal working schedule of an enterprise.

2. Which of the following is the advantage of audit? (　　)

    A. Disputes among the managerial personnel are easier to resolve.

    B. Major changes in the ownership may be facilitated if the past accounts contain an unqualified auditing report.

    C. Auditing can help third parties obtain more fair information.

    D. All of the above.

3. Which one of the following is included in the planning stage? (　　)

    A. Making audit target.   B. Risk assessment.

    C. Testing of internal control.   D. Audit report.

4. Which one of the following is included in the auditing implementation stage? (　　)

    A. Making audit target.   B. Making audit scope.

    C. Making audit content.   D. Making risk assessment.

5. Which one of the following is the final stage of audit? (　　)

    A. Help the customer improve profits.

    B. Express an opinion on the financial statements.

    C. Give advice on the strategy of customers.

    D. Help to enhance internal control.

6. Which of the following is not a fundamental principle? (　　)

    A. Effectiveness.   B. Integrity.

    C. Objectivity.   D. Confidentiality.

7. Which of the following is not a threat to independence? (　　)

    A. Self-review threat.   B. Advocacy threat.

    C. Familiarity threat.   D. Unprofessional threat.

8. Which of the following is not an element of internal control? (   )

    A. Control environment.   B. Risk assessment.

    C. Control procedure.   D. Professional behavior.

9. Which of the following is the reflection of the whole audit process during the audit of financial statements of Certified Public Accountants? (   )

    A. The audit working paper.   B. Audit target.

    C. The quality of audit work.   D. Code of professional ethics.

10. All of the following are objectives of internal control except (   ).

    A. maximize net income   B. comply with legal requirements

    C. safeguard assets   D. reliable accounting records

11. What is the classification of audit?

12. What is the process of auditing?

13. Make an evaluation of this sentence "Audits can help companies maximize profits" and state your opinion with explanation.